Myths, Metaphors, and Science Fiction

Conversation Pieces

A Small Paperback Series from Aqueduct Press
Subscriptions available: www.aqueductpress.com

About the Aqueduct Press
Conversation Pieces Series

The feminist engaged with sf is passionately interested in challenging the way things are, passionately determined to understand how everything works. It is my constant sense of our feminist-sf present as a grand conversation that enables me to trace its existence into the past and from there see its trajectory extending into our future. A genealogy for feminist sf would not constitute a chart depicting direct lineages but would offer us an ever-shifting, fluid mosaic, the individual tiles of which we will probably only ever partially access. What could be more in the spirit of feminist sf than to conceptualize a genealogy that explicitly manifests our own communities across not only space but also time?

Aqueduct's small paperback series, Conversation Pieces, aims to both document and facilitate the "grand conversation." The Conversation Pieces series presents a wide variety of texts, including short fiction (which may not always be sf and may not necessarily even be feminist), essays, speeches, manifestoes, poetry, interviews, correspondence, and group discussions. Many of the texts are reprinted material, but some are new. The grand conversation reaches at least as far back as Mary Shelley and extends, in our speculations and visions, into the continually-created future. In Jonathan Goldberg's words, "To look forward to the history that will be, one must look at and retell the history that has been told." And that is what Conversation Pieces is all about.

L. Timmel Duchamp

Jonathan Goldberg, "The History That Will Be" in Louise Fradenburg and Carla Freccero, eds., *Premodern Sexualities* (New York and London: Routledge, 1996)

Published by Aqueduct Press
PO Box 95787
Seattle, WA 98145-2787
www.aqueductpress.com

ISBN: 978-1-61976-055-4

Publication history: "Fantastic Voyages" appeared in a slightly different version as "Fantastic Journeys of the Mythic Kind," in *James Gunn's Ad Astra*, Issue 1, July 2012;
"Of Myth and Memory" appeared in *SFWA Bulletin*, April 2014.

Cover illustration: The Eagle Has Risen: Stellar Spire in the Eagle Nebula; NASA, ESA, and The Hubble Heritage Team (STScI/AURA)

Original Block Print of Mary Shelley by Justin Kempton: www.writersmugs.com

Printed in the USA by Applied Digital Imaging

Conversation Pieces
Volume 39

Myths, Metaphors, and Science Fiction

Ancient Roots of the Literature of the Future

by
Sheila Finch

Acknowledgments

I first fell under the spell of mythology as a child in a post-World War II elementary school in London, listening to weekly BBC school broadcasts about the Greeks and the Trojans, their gods and their adventures. Later, wise teachers showed me these same heroic figures in the plays of Shakespeare. So you can imagine how thrilled I was later to read science fiction and find these old friends alive and well in Outer Space. I wish I could go back and thank those teachers!

Once again, I thank my friends and colleagues of the Asilomar Writing Consortium, without whose unfailing support and inspiration I would achieve far, far less: especially, Rose Hamilton-Gottlieb, Jon Russ, Barry Slater, Dan Houston-Davila, Grant Farley, Kendall Evans, Samantha Henderson, Harry Lowther, Natalie Hirt, Dave and Mary Putnam, Deborah Kolodji, Susan Vreeland, and AWC's founder, Jerry Hannah.

I also wish to thank Stephen Klein, Librarian Extraordinaire at the Los Angeles County Library, for always managing to find out-of-print books and sources that eluded me.

And special thanks to my editors at Aqueduct Press, particularly Kath Wilham who saved me from embarrassing myself many times over.

For

Shannon, Kyle, Austin, Autumn, Douglas, Christopher,
Amy, Erynn, and Tyler

"Metaphoric thinking is fundamental to our understanding of the world, because it is the *only* way in which understanding can reach outside the systems of signs to life itself. It is what links language to life."

Iain McGilchrist, *The Master and His Emissary*

"These ancient stories have a great deal to tell us…partly because meaning in mythology is so compressed. They allow you to dive in and unpack them."

Salman Rushdie, speaking about *Midnight's Children*

"Religions, philosophies, arts, the social forms of primitive and historic man, prime discoveries in science and technology, the very dreams that blister sleep, boil up from the basic, magic ring of myth."

Joseph Campbell, *The Hero with a Thousand Faces*

Contents

Introduction

Humankind has been telling and re-telling mythic tales for tens of thousands of years; all around the globe we find recognizable themes and archetypes. It shouldn't surprise us that contemporary stories that affect us powerfully—including science fiction stories—have their roots in this rich mother lode. Myths (and fairy tales) are neither true nor false. Besides their entertainment value, they are psychological metaphors for the human condition and frequently teaching tools too. Myths that purport to tell the stories of gods and immortals are concerned with defining what makes us human. While our formidable brains are capable of marvelous feats of logic and analysis, there remains a vast ocean of experience that we can access only obliquely through our emotions and our intuition, and metaphor is the language we employ to do this. The great myths seek to explain us to ourselves—our exploits, passions, triumphs, and failures. They can be found all over the world, often displaying remarkable similarity.

Nobody—scientist, seer, or science fiction writer—can reliably predict what will happen two days from now, let alone two millennia. Science fiction is really about us as humans—living, loving, fighting, raising families—but set in another place and time so that the message may get through without being censored by the self-protective function of our egos. The scenery and gadgets are fun to contemplate, the dilemmas posed sometimes thrilling and sometimes terrifying, but in the end, the stories are about humans facing new kinds of challenges and how they change or are changed by their environment.

It may sound like heresy at first, to say it doesn't matter whether we think this imagined environment is actually possible or not. In the case of novels like George Orwell's *1984* (published, 1949), which now looks like some kind of failed prophecy, or stories about aliens on Mars in Roger Zelazny's "A Rose for Ecclesiastes" (1963), where even the author knew it was *not* possible, we appreciate such stories according to what we learn from them about what it means to be human, now and in the future. To understand the difference, take a look at Hugo Gernsback's *Ralph 24C1 4C1+*, first published in 1911. (Today's texting generation can probably understand that faster than Gernsback's original readers!) The man who gave his name to one of science fiction's greatest prizes created a cast of characters who are basically touring the future and gawking at technology, not much else. We get a catalog of gosh! wow! inventions that strike us today as either quaint or amusing ("Helio-Dynamophores" for solar power; "Signalizers," searchlights mounted on tall buildings to guide aircraft; the "Bacillatorium" where germs were eliminated from human bodies by means of a "Radio-arcturium" cathode). The result is an unmemorable story where practically the only pleasure we can derive from reading it today is counting the number of future inventions Gernsback got wrong. What matters is whether the story gives precedence to the glittering gadgets or to the humanity of the characters, and we should judge the importance of the work of both male and female authors by this standard.

The question arises whether the use of, or reference to, or intimation of, ancient myth is conscious on the part of the writers, whether the borrowing is deliberate or accidental; and the answer I think is sometimes yes, sometimes no. The end result seems to me to be the same. Damon Knight once said that the shortest definition of a short story is "something changes for somebody," and added that sometimes the "somebody" is the reader. Through the medium of the modern mythic tale we call "science fiction," we ourselves are changed. It's not important whether or not the author was consciously acting as the "man behind the curtain."

This collection is not intended as an exhaustive examination of the subject; for the most part, I've restricted the discussion of myths to Graeco-Roman ones because these are the ones western readers may be familiar with already. And I deliberately haven't undertaken a discussion of fantasy and fairy tales, where the elements of myth are usually plainly visible, except in places where I hope it might ease the reader's introduction to what may seem very odd concepts. Similarly I've occasionally referred to, or briefly discussed, familiar mainstream literature or popular movies. And in some of these essays, we'll stray off the strictly mythic path to look at themes that seem more like racial memories: stories that, while not strictly about gods and magical beings, nevertheless make use of timeless metaphors and have their roots deep in the past.

Besides the obviously long shadow of Carl Gustav Jung over this work, two other scholars of myth, legend, and fairy tale have influenced my thinking: Joseph Campbell (I recommend starting with *The Hero with a Thousand Faces* [1949], which is not as extreme in its speculation as some of his other work) and Bruno Bettelheim. I would be remiss if I didn't also name Mircea

Eliade and Claude Lévi-Strauss, whose studies were also invaluable to this work.

I don't intend to suggest that a successful story follows the outline of any particular myth without deviation. And obviously, not every story published as science fiction contains mythic roots or even mythic themes. But I'm convinced that such roots contribute to the emotional power of a story, making it harder to forget. Ours is a scientific age; we pride ourselves on having outgrown the superstitions of our grandparents, but Jung and Campbell remind us of something much deeper than the intellect, bright though its light shining on our world may be. I want to examine that odd, inexplicable moment we sometimes have when viewing sacred art or reading poetry or perhaps just contemplating a particularly awesome sunset, when we sense a connection to—

What, exactly?

Something, evidently, even though we can't put a name to it. We call this shiver of recognition, the "numinous," and these essays are an attempt to track when it occurs in science fiction.

Sheila Finch
Long Beach, CA, 2014

Of Myth and Memory

A few years ago, after hearing Ray Bradbury speak at a session of UC Riverside's Eaton Conference, I picked up a copy of *Dandelion Wine* (1957), replacing my original copy lost many moves earlier. I looked forward to reacquainting myself with a classic example of his work. I wasn't disappointed. The experience caused me to re-examine just what it is in a piece of literature that captures me, what makes a story unforgettable and moving, beyond the surface levels of plot, or good writing, or even believable characters.

I was introduced to Bradbury long ago by a twelve-year-old boy whose parents were visiting on their way up the California coast. We were living in San Luis Obispo at the time, and friends traveling between Los Angeles and San Francisco frequently took a break halfway at our house. The boy's parents and my husband were musicians, and when he and I found ourselves left out of their very technical conversation, we began to talk about books and learned we were both avid readers. As our guests were leaving, he gave me his paperback copy of *The Illustrated Man* (1951), which he'd finished reading on the family trip—highly recommended, he said. I didn't recognize the name of the book or its author, but since I'm addicted to reading at bedtime and had run out of things to read, I turned to his offering. The rest is history, as they say. I fell in love with Bradbury's voice as much as the stories themselves, saturating myself in his music. Bradbury's prose is poetry, and best read aloud.

In fact, I realized, as I re-visited these stories of life in a vanished time and place in America, that it's not the story itself that grabs me and never was. Most of the stories have sparse plots that would sound ho-hum if summarized in a sentence or two. And the characters, the innocent children and wise old adults that populate the pages, probably had few counterparts, even in Bradbury's own childhood in Illinois. But that's not really the point. The magic of these stories lies in the fact that they're metaphors, translating Bradbury's personal memories into transcendent myth.

Of course, I'm not the first to remark that so many Bradbury lines enchant the ear out of all proportion to the information they actually carry. Consider the opening paragraph of the first "chapter" (Bradbury doesn't name or number them as such) in *Dandelion Wine*:

> It was a quiet morning, the town covered over with darkness and at ease in bed. Summer gathered in the weather, the wind had the proper touch, the breathing of the world was long and warm and slow. You had only to rise, lean from your window, and know that this indeed was the first real time of freedom and living, this was the first morning of summer. (p. 1)

Here's another opening:

> And then there is that day when all around, all around you hear the dropping of the apples, one by one from the trees. At first it is one here and one there, and then it is three and then it is four and then nine and twenty, until all the apples plummet like rain, fall like horse hoofs in the

soft, darkening grass, and you see the last apple on the tree, and you wait for the wind to work you slowly free from your hold upon the sky and drop you down and down…. (p. 129)

A lesser writer might have written, "It was an early summer morning," for the first, and "In Autumn, when apples fall from the trees" for the second—and would've missed the dreamlike world that Bradbury's words create, a world we immediately recognize as true to our own mythic childhood. My childhood passed in wartime London, crowded, grubby, dangerous, and certainly lacking apple trees, but that image is emotionally more real to me than broken paving stones and dusty privet bushes and the sound of air raid sirens. The poet T. S. Eliot called that careful selection of pictures to evoke emotional recognition, the "objective correlative," the image that opens up the whole experience for us (1921, p. 3). Bradbury's Spring and Autumn are the way the seasons *should be* in childhood, not the way they actually may be. Nor can we avoid the poetic transfer of subject that occurs from the Narrator observing the fall of the apples to the Narrator becoming the apples themselves, surely a mythic transformation!

I re-read the book with a great deal of pleasure, recognizing the parts I'd admired before when I knew so much less about the skill that lies behind the apparently effortless ability of simple words to stir emotion. Bradbury, like all the best poets, makes it seem easy. And that realization brought me to remember the words of another poet I've always loved, whose work is a rhapsody about simple places and simple people: Dylan Thomas.

I hadn't read *Under Milk Wood* (1954), a radio play, in a very long time, though I re-read Thomas's collected poems at least once a year. I remember hating twentieth century poetry while I was in high school, until I encountered Richard Burton's reading of Thomas's poem "Fern Hill." For the first time, I had the experience of being swept away by the emotional torrent of images, with only the slightest understanding of what the poem meant. The American poet Archibald MacLeish was speaking of this experience when he wrote, "A poem should not mean/But be" (1926).

Like Bradbury, Thomas loved childhood and small towns, though his are in his native Wales:

> …herring gulls heckling down to the harbour where the fishermen spit and prop the morning up and eye the fishy sea smooth to the sea's end as it lulls in blue. Green and gold money, tobacco, tinned salmon, hats with feathers, pots of fish-paste, warmth for the winter-to-be, weave and leap in it rich and slippery in the flash and shapes of fishes through the cold sea-streets.
> | (p. 50)

I've never lived in towns anything like either poet describes, yet I seem to remember them; the music of the words conjures them in my imagination. How real those men propping up the morning! How vivid the smell of the herring flashing under the cold waves! I have no childhood memory of a place like that—how could I? Yet I know its seasons intimately. Here's another example:

> It is spring, moonless night in the small town, starless and bible-black, the cobblestreets silent and the hunched, courters'-and-rabbits' wood limping invisible down to the sloeblack, slow, black, crowblack, fishing-boat bobbing sea. (p. 1)

The thing is, these aren't memories of the places where Bradbury and Thomas spent their childhoods either. These visions are dreams, metaphors their au-

8

thors have constructed about remembered places, and as such they're truer than bricks and stones. We may call them "mythic." Myths and dreams arise from the unconscious, and their insights are not analyzable by daytime logic; they're neither true nor false. The neuroscientist Iain McGilchrist tells us in *The Master and His Emissary* (2009), "Metaphoric thinking is fundamental to our understanding of the world. It is what links language to life." The powerful emotional reaction such images provoke, a response to the numinous long before intellectual understanding takes place, is the hallmark of myth. And thus, through poetry—a language our hearts respond to even when our brains have difficulty understanding the words—they remake our own memories into something richer and more meaningful.

That's all very well, you may be thinking, but is this effect possible to achieve in a far-future story, something more hard-core than Bradbury's visions? Consider this scene from C. L. Moore's short story "No Woman Born" (1944), in which a lover first sees the rebuilt, robotic body of his beloved who almost perished in a devastating fire:

> She stood quietly, letting the heavy mailed folds of her garment settle about her. They fell together with a faint ringing sound, like small bells far off, and hung beautifully in pale golden, sculptured folds…. She swayed just a bit, vitality burning inextinguishably in her brain as it once had burned in her body…. The golden garment caught points of light from the fire and glimmered at him with tiny reflections as she moved…like Phoenix from the fire. (p. 160)

We might never have imagined that a cyborg could be so hauntingly lovely, but Catherine Moore refers to the mythical golden bird arising re-born from the con-suming fire, and poetic images ("small bells far off," "points of light from the fire…glimmered ") to make a possible future situation—and a bizarre one at that—at once vivid and moving. Something we may never have thought about previously, we now find we respond to on a deep level.

The more we study the literature of science fic-tion, ostensibly a collection of dreams and nightmares about possible futures, the more we come to realize that it gains much of its emotional power to move us through the myths it embodies and re-creates. We may not consciously recognize these elements, charmed and distracted as we are by the surface components of next-generation technologies and the conflicts and quanda-ries they may bring. Robots and starships and quantum worlds are exciting to those of us who love to speculate about "coming attractions" (as Fritz Leiber might have called them), but in the best examples of the field there's more going on than just a display of the author's fer-tile imagination of possibilities. This is the realm of the numinous that Carl Gustav Jung speaks of, that deep tug at our emotions, that odd thrill of something other-worldly, transcendent. We can't explain it—and would probably deny it if we could—for it surpasses our con-scious understanding, perhaps *bypasses* it, evoking echoes of forgotten mysteries.

It seems to me that the way to unlock the full trea-sure of the stories told by writers such as Bradbury and Moore is by giving ourselves up to the poetry, the rhythms, alliterations, images, and metaphors, by recog-nizing their underlying myths and allowing ourselves to respond to them. In even the hardest of "hard sf," with its emphasis on science and technology, its exploration of troubling and important questions, it's the underlying resonance of these ancient themes that gives the best work its timeless quality.

Fantastic Voyages

The word "hero" is over-used and misused today. It has come to describe the entertainer who is the object of teen crushes and the sports star who wins the cup for the fans, as well as more deserving firefighters rushing to save the baby from the burning building, or doctors and nurses working twenty-four hours at a stretch to help the victims of some unimaginable disaster. Yet none of these are what Homer had in mind when he wrote what became the definitive account of the making of a Hero.

Homer's account of Odysseus's wanderings in the Mediterranean on the way home from the siege of Troy is probably the most important myth underlying all western fiction, let alone science fiction. Versions of this story are found in virtually all of the world's mythologies, their details surprisingly similar; we know it as The Hero's Journey. Its account of the Greek king's dangerous adventures, the enemies, helpers—human and supernatural—tricksters and seducers he meets along the way, offers a metaphor for the trials and tribulations of human life, the yearning for a long-lost Eden of home, the triumph of the human spirit over adversity. But our fascination with voyaging certainly predates Homer. We're born with wanderlust; the lure of the long migration out of Africa is in our blood. When we're prevented from voyaging in person, by finances or health or circumstance, we have always turned to the next best thing, the tales of other explorers' adventures. *The Odyssey* is the bedrock and archetype for all such tales, whether mainstream or science fiction.

Joseph Campbell codified the Hero's Journey (the "plot," as it were) from mythic versions found around the world as follows: The Hero's birth and background are unknown, but rumor suggests at least one royal parent; he grows up in obscurity, but is called to undertake a quest to save the kingdom. At first, he's reluctant to accept, but a mentor appears and offers counsel and training. He sets out on this journey, and by a series of trials including a near-death descent into the underworld, and aided by both human and non-human spirits or animal helpers, he eventually prevails and gains the goal. On his return, he is hailed a conquering hero. In some expanded versions of the myth, this acclaim is fleeting, and a few years later, he is attacked by his erstwhile followers and dies, after which his reputation grows; he is revered and sometimes accepted as a god, or at least the founder of a cult. All mythic Heroes share the majority of these indicators. Among them, Campbell points out, we find Orpheus and Osiris, Odysseus, Moses, Gautama Sakyamuni, and Jesus; in science fiction the most obvious example is Luke Skywalker. George Lucas, creator of *Star Wars* (1977), has said he consciously based both the central character and his mission, along with a couple of very non-human helpers, on Campbell's analysis of the myth. Predating Lucas's use of the myth, we find Poul Anderson's "Goat Song" (1960), a complex—and conscious—science fictional retelling of the Orpheus version of the story, with a computer called SUM in the place of the god of the underworld. The last two examples represent conscious use of the myth by an author, but that isn't important; what matters is the effect on the reader.

Heroes don't necessarily fit all the categories Campbell identified. Some, like the Hobbits in J. R. R. Tolkien's fantasy saga *The Lord of the Rings* (1954) may not be royal but are definitely called out of obscurity to go on a quest fraught with difficulties and dangers, and after prevailing, return to obscurity—but profoundly changed, deepened. This variation of the "hero from obscurity" is prevalent in science fiction.

We need to take up one issue before we go further. Homer's Hero is male, and we're going to find that most (but not all) characters in science fiction that embark on the Hero's Journey are male. Similarly, most authors (but not all) of such stories are male. The female counterpart of the myth of Odysseus is the myth of Demeter and Persephone, which we'll take up next. And again, it bears repeating that sometimes female authors use the male myth as a template (with male or female characters in that role) and sometimes male authors use the female myth in similar fashion.

There are two aspects to the theme of fantastic voyages: the journey itself, with all its hardships, adventures and entertainments, and second, the quest, the reason the voyage is undertaken in the first place. "Journey" stories are mainly about the privations and dangers along the way, scarcely concerning themselves with the projected outcome of the voyage, often ending when the far shore is reached. (In film, we find "Road" stories—two good buddies on a trip—fit this definition.) "Quest" stories, on the other hand, give fewer details of the trek or of life onboard the ship, the journey being necessary only to get the characters to the goal. We can think of the account of John Glenn's first orbit of the Earth as being one of the first kind of stories, Neil Armstrong's setting foot on the Moon as an example of the second.

Journey and goal are frequently so interrelated that it becomes difficult to talk about one without considering the other. An early short story, Alan Nourse's "Brightside Crossing" (1951), gives us an example of the difficulty of separating out these two aspects of fantastic voyage stories. The journey theme in Nourse's story comes from a small group of scientist/adventurers trekking across Mercury's hellish landscape, as the first westerner to make the summit of Everest said about climbing the mountain, "because it's there." But the central character's desire to return to a trek that almost killed him reveals the importance of the goal, at least to the main character: the human conquest of a hostile planet.

When we're dealing with a multi-volume story such as the *Lord of the Rings* saga, apart from the over-arching focus of the series, all the books except the last can be seen as journey stories; only the last, the climax, is obviously a matter of the goal. The adventures encountered by the little band on their fantastic journey are moving and full of meaning, but they cannot be fully appreciated without the goal of the one ring's retrieval at the end of the cycle. (Tolkien was both consciously using myth in this saga of the fight of Good with Evil and inventing new themes.) Though the first volumes in the saga can be understood as journey stories, the overall story is ultimately a quest of the highest importance, like the story of Parsifal, an attempt to save or redeem the world. What's important in differentiating the two types is this central focus.

For the purpose of clarity, we'll consider the two parts of this myth separately as they appear in science fiction narratives.

The Journey

The *Odyssey* is certainly the mythic root of all subsequent Western travel tales. It encompasses battles, perilous escapes, dangerous situations, horrifying monsters, acts of courage and acts of treachery, the temptations of sexual attraction, the strangeness of the universe in ancient Greek terms; these are elements that lend themselves easily to science fiction narratives. Odysseus himself displays many—but not all—of the characteristics of the Hero; for instance, his lineage though royal is not unknown, but he is called out of a pastoral and domestic existence to take part in the rescue of the abducted Helen. Myths always contain an instructive subtext. Odysseus's ten-year voyage illustrates the importance of faithfulness to a goal, self-reliance, strength of character, spiritual growth, and the encounter with other cultures and other ways of being. It's important to note that the lengthy account ends once Odysseus's faithful old dog recognizes him, and he clears out Penelope's hundred suitors to reclaim his kingdom. The journey itself was the point of the story. (There is a lesser-known version of the myth in which the story has a kind of coda in which Odysseus is brought to face what he has learned from his voyaging, as if the Greek poet is making certain his audience gets the point.)

We humans are born susceptible to wanderlust. Over time, vast numbers of humans have shown a willingness to risk their lives on voyages of exploration, often taking artifacts of their culture with them. In the fifteenth century Chinese voyages of discovery, thousands of non-sailors were aboard the junks, including diplomats, concubines, and Buddhist priests. (For an introduction to these voyages, see Menzies' *1421,* published in 2004.) Nor was this solely an Oriental custom; Sugden's biography of Sir Francis Drake (1990) tells us that the *Golden Hind*, sailing around the world in the sixteenth century, provided musicians as well as a parson. Today's cruise passengers expect food, medical care, sometimes even spiritual counseling; games and other recreations are all part of the journey, and romance frequently is included in the package.

Film-makers have made good use of this theme of futuristic voyages, the most obvious example being Arthur C. Clarke's *2001*. Both the 1968 film and the book carry the subtitle "A Space Odyssey" in case we miss the mythic connection of this dangerous journey across our own solar system. It ends enigmatically with the birth of the Star Child, certainly not a goal the journey's planners could have foreseen or aimed for. The film and television series *Star Trek,* first appearing in 1966, offers another example. The *Enterprise* becomes a world unto itself on its long voyages; romances are not uncommon (although if they involve Captain Kirk, they're destined to end unhappily). Later iterations of the series even have elaborate entertainment features such as the holodeck on board for the crew to while away the long time between ports-of-call. The emotional and psychological effect of the voyage on the voyagers is often a prominent part of the plot. Since significant portions of each episode take place on the ship, we can consider *Star Trek* a modern Odyssey, a story where the voyage itself is at least as important as the outcome, much like tv's western series *Wagon Train* (1957-62), itself a version of the Hero's Journey, from which *Star Trek* derives.

To my mind, the purest example of a fantastic journey, where the strangeness of the voyage *is* the story, occurs in Norman Spinrad's novel *The Void Captain's Tale* (1983). No priest or parson on the ships of Spinrad's fictional cruise line, but cruise directors and the entertainment they provide make for a vivid sub-plot. Unshackled from what Spinrad terms the "quotidian world," the passengers engage in bizarre behaviors and sexual rituals. In fact, the novel describes in some detail the culture of customs and recreation that develops on ships of the Second Starfaring Age:

> The "lowest" deck of the Grand Palais module was given over to a seemingly chaotic maze of dream chambers opening off a convoluted tunneled passageway that curved and wound around them…. The organically rounded walls of the tunnel glowed an erotic rose, a hue picked up and made palpable by the perfumed mist that filled it. Many of the chambers were already occupied…the sighs and moans, the rhythmic rustlings, were allowed to suffuse into the rosy ambiance of the passageway, surrounding us with the music d'amour. (p. 44)

Like Odysseus, Genro Kane Gupta, the Void Captain of Spinrad's tale, is a basically good man who finds himself sexually tempted and in considerable danger of losing both his life and his soul on a very strange voyage. The resonant echo of the ancient myth is what draws the reader in so powerfully to this future tale. Science fiction has long explored the idea of the generation ships that will be needed for truly long voyages in space, absent the discovery of FTL drives or stargates. What Spinrad's novel illustrates is that our culture will change with and be changed by the journey itself. New Earth won't be much like Old Earth. Customs we probably can't even dream about will have evolved, certainly new fashions, new cuisine, new laws. No ancient myth could be expected to forecast them. But basic human dilemmas of right and wrong-doing that Homer would've recognized will remain.

The late twentieth century Blue Tyson series of novels by Australian writer Terry Dowling develops Homer's theme with a wind-driven ship that crosses the desert of the near-future Australian Outback. Like the Hero archetype, Dowling's protagonist, Tom Rynosseros, a man with a mysterious past, is called to undertake a desperate and dangerous adventure that will determine more than the fate of the central characters, and in doing so he encounters fantastic creatures, aliens, and artificial intelligences. That this intersection of myth and science fiction is conscious on Dowling's part is underscored by an epigraph from Jung that he chose for *Blue Tyson*, the first book in the series (1992):

> This is the task always…not to illuminate the ancient truths, the ancient intimations of the unconscious, the ancient intimations of the soul, but…to make them immediate and contemporary, to give them meaning in the here and now. (p. v)

It's striking when we find that the myth of the perilous odyssey is the pattern underlying a hard science fiction narrative, and particularly so when the writer has the scientific credentials of Gregory Benford. Yet *Great Sky River* (1987) and its sequel *Tides of Light* (1989) are at heart the story of a small band of humans forced to flee alien pursuers, embarking on a fantastic journey to hoped-for sanctuary at the center of our galaxy. Since the overall destiny of Killeen and the band of fugitives he leads isn't met in either of these books, they can be considered examples of journey stories, with the full complement of harrowing dangers, exotic creatures (some of whom are helpers), nightmare landscapes, and descents into "hell" that appear in the original myth. That a twenty-first century reader can empathize with the plight of augmented future humans on worlds that bear no physical resemblance to our own Earth is due not only to the author's persuasive powers of description but also to the emotional resonance of the underlying myth. Benford frequently uses imagery that makes reference to recognizable human emotional reactions (T. S. Eliot's "objective correlative"), thus grounding the reader in the midst of very alien scenery and events. In *Great Sky River* we read:

> They popped helmets…and kissed in incredulous greeting. Only taste and touch were trusted now, the human press of warm and pungent flesh. Killeen breathed in the rank running-smell of Sanhakan. Then the slightly muskier odor of a woman who was suddenly at his elbow…. Another woman, old and weathered, smelling of salty exertion…. (p. 80)

This is what Eliot meant: The use of the sense of smell here, especially the smell of sweat, serves to make the imagined future meeting, with all its danger and poignancy, come alive for the reader so that we do not merely understand, we experience. We respond to the plot on a deep level, but we've never seen it told like this before.

Earlier examples, where the journey has more words devoted to it than the arrival, include several Jules Verne stories, especially *Twenty Thousand Leagues Under the Sea* (1870). In this tale, which might as well be a voyage into outer space, Captain Nemo (whose name is an allusion to Odysseus's answer to the challenge to give his name: "No man") pilots the submarine *Nautilus* through a vast seascape of natural and scientific wonders. A. E. Van

Vogt's *Voyage of the Space Beagle* (1950) and Poul Anderson's *Tau Zero* (1970) fit in this category too. Another early story, Stanley Weinbaum's "A Martian Odyssey" (1934) picks up Homer's theme of comparative ethnology, the clash of alien encounters, where Jarvis, the human explorer, meets and learns to deal with "Tweel," a representative of the dominant race on Mars. Reading these modern versions of the mythic voyage, we see that rather than being simply Tourists-in-Space travelogues, the best of them entail extreme jeopardy for the voyagers on their fantastic journeys, and, like Homer's tale, opportunities for spiritual growth.

A new author who has incorporated the structure of the Hero's Journey is G. Willow Wilson. In *Alif the Unseen* (2012), we encounter a young Arab-Indian computer hacker living in an unspecified Islamic world in the present. Like the traditional Hero, Alif (his adopted name) is a nonentity in his society, called to fight a greater evil than the privacy concerns of his clients. He is reluctant to do so, but is aided by others along the way, including his neighbor Dina and a Djinn called Vikram. (Since the Djinns are described here as being an Elder Race, created before the Human one, they may have special powers but are not supernatural beings as might traditionally be found in the Hero's Journey—and thus the book remains science fiction.) Alif faces his own trials, such as life-threatening events and betrayals. And in a nod to the domestic end of Odysseus's saga, he returns home with the promise of marriage to Dina.

Other women writers who have incorporated parts or all of this journey theme into their work include Leigh Brackett, C.L. Moore, and C.J. Cherryh. A character moving through an unknown landscape, facing hardships and having adventures on the way to a goal, provides the framework to many stories. Ursula Le Guin's novel *A*

Wizard of Earthsea (1968), while obviously not fitting our category of hard sf, illustrates this, as does her definitely science fiction novel *The Left Hand of Darkness* (1969), where Genly Ai commutes between opposing capitals in Karhide and Orgoreyn, finally culminating in an epic ice journey. But we mustn't forget that categorizing a story as being a version of the Hero's Journey without recognizing the importance and weight of the other themes it contains is to do it an injustice, no matter the sex or gender of the author.

The Quest

As part of his advice on writing, Robert Heinlein proposed that only three basic plots are available to writers: Romeo and Juliet, The Man Who Learned Better, and The Little Tailor. This is a bit of oversimplification on Heinlein's part, but it should be immediately obvious that all three of the categories he identifies are themselves based on archetypes such as we've been discussing. The one that concerns us here is The Little Tailor's story, a fairy tale journey in which a character sets out to gain a boon for himself or for his society. In myths, the one on the quest seeks the rescue of someone abducted (Helen of Troy), or a magic object (Jason and the Golden Fleece); in legends, it might be the Holy Grail that will cure the ailing king and his suffering kingdom (a lot of the King Arthur cycle); in fairy tales, it is the hand of the king's daughter (the Little Tailor). If the voyage itself is strange enough, we might be treated to the main character's adventures along the way, but the real meat and the true focus comes when he confronts the dragons that literally or figuratively guard the treasure. Whether the outcome of the quest is successful or not doesn't affect the emotional resonance of the underlying myth, though readers of science fiction tend to value optimism more often than not.

In one sense, the vast majority of all science fiction stories—perhaps western fiction in general—are quest stories; the major character has a goal to achieve and obstacles to overcome on the path toward that achievement. This may reflect how deep the influence of mythic structure lies in our response to fiction. In many mainstream stories, the quest is a purely psychological one, what Heinlein might have labeled "man who learns better" stories. However, in science fiction, "mythic quest" stories entail a physical journey across other landscapes than the one we know, even when the focus is on the boon at the end.

When I considered journey stories, I remarked on the details of the voyagers' culture that emerge and evolve, the emphasis on what might be called landscapes and adventures along the way, and a plot that frequently terminates with the arrival at the destination. The quest story, by contrast, emphasizes the struggle for the goal, often at great cost to the main character. A clear and important example of this occurs in Mary Doria Russell's *The Sparrow* (1996). Not only is the long voyage from Earth to the planet from which radio signals have been picked up hardly described beyond basic details— hollowed out asteroid, hydroponic agriculture—but life on Earth to which the sole survivor, an obscure Jesuit priest, returns decades later hasn't changed that much beyond a few technological advances (compare this to Odysseus's return to an almost time-locked court). The heart of the story is about the goal of the mission: first, to meet, interact with and understand an alien culture, and second to survive the nightmarish experience and bring the knowledge gained back to Earth. In the process, the priest, Emilio Sandoz, suffers greatly, very nearly loses his life along with the rest of the expedition's members, and undergoes a profound crisis of faith in his own version of the descent into the underworld where he finds himself "an exact counterpart of a capuchin monkey kept on a golden chain by some sixteenth century European aristocrat" (p. 389), with the added horror of physical mutilation and sexual assault.

It may not appear at first that Sandoz is very heroic, and it's difficult to see what boon he brings back to Earth from this terrifying mission, but this becomes clear when we consider words from the novel's opening: "The Jesuit scientists went to learn, not to proselytize. They went so that they might come to know and love God's other children…. They meant no harm" (p. 5). In the harsh interrogation Sandoz is subjected to on his return by his own order—a further reference to the later, bitter experience of the mythic hero—we are brought to understand that it sometimes takes heroic effort just to survive, an effort that isn't always successful but is a human duty to undertake. Frightful knowledge gained is better than comfortable ignorance indulged.

Other examples of quest narratives include Hal Clement's *Mission of Gravity* (1954), where the alien Barlennan takes on the extraordinary dangers of his home planet, Meskline, to rescue a lost human rocket probe. But more than this, Barlennan is inspired to undertake this quest by the opportunity to expand his knowledge. In Le Guin's *The Left Hand of Darkness* the Human envoy, Genly Ai, comes to Gethen to make diplomatic contact with its hermaphroditic inhabitants, for whom he has at first scant empathy; the tale ends in a harrowing ice journey of escape with one of them during which he gains understanding of and compassion for the Gethenians to an extent far greater than he could have anticipated when setting out on his original quest. This psychological growth is the hallmark of the Hero's Journey.

Eliade remarks that:

> in modern societies the prose narrative, especially the novel has taken the place of the recitation of myths in traditional and popular societies…. This is especially true in regard to the initiatory theme, the theme of the ordeals of the Hero-Redeemer. (p. 191)

He might as well have been talking about science fiction.

It may turn out that we have already made enough preliminary voyages into space, learned enough from robotic probe and piloted shuttle to know how long and how repetitious in terms of event such long journeys inevitably are; perhaps the reader will grow tired of fantastic journey tales. I suspect the literary future will lie with the quest version of this myth.

Wild Women and the Way Inside

What are we supposed to think Penelope was doing, all those long years when her husband Odysseus was wandering around the Mediterranean having adventures? We're told she was weaving, and unraveling the work every night to keep the hundred suitors at bay. It doesn't say much for the suitors' intellectual caliber if they never figured out that ruse! But the story underlines something we should look into next: women's mythic themes differ from men's. As we've seen, this is not to say that the great myths don't interest or affect women, because of course they do. One check of the number of female sf authors who have used what we might now call the "male myth" of the Hero's Journey with both male and female protagonists should put that notion to rest. Penelope's story points to the difference in the weight given to the two aspects of life. We might label the journeys undertaken as the active (outward directed) and the contemplative (inward directed).

The primal female myth is the story of Demeter, the daughter of Kronos, one of the Elder Gods deposed by Zeus and company. As the goddess of fertility and agriculture, Demeter probably represents a very old female corn deity, going back to humanity's first forays into growing food and harvesting; her story is known in one form or another all over the Middle East and as far away as Asia. If the crops don't grow and prosper, if the harvest isn't plentiful, people will die. It's a simple concept that we understand even today; the link with human fertility is also obvious.

Demeter had a daughter of whom she was extremely fond, Persephone. At first, according to the myth, all was well. Demeter presided over fruitful harvests and her people were well fed. But one day as she and her beautiful daughter were walking through the flowering landscape, Hades, King of the Underworld, happened to see them. Instantly, he fell in love and was determined to have Persephone as his queen. Over Demeter's protests, he abducted her daughter to live with him as his consort in the land of death. The distraught mother withdrew her benign oversight of the land, and the resulting year-round winter allowed no seeds to sprout, no crops to grow, no harvests to feed the suffering people. Obviously, a sterile, untenable condition! Eventually, the lamentations of goddess and people reached Zeus's ears, and a compromise was worked out with Hades. Persephone was to spend half the year in the kingdom of the dead with her husband, half with her mother among the living. And Demeter promised that in the period that her daughter was with her, the flowers and crops would grow and the harvests would be fruitful. When Persephone went back to Hades, winter reigned on the Earth.

Out of this myth grew a cult of female priests and a ceremonial observation of mysteries anchored to the Demeter/Persephone story, practiced mostly by women—though men did take part—named from the place where Demeter's temple was established. The Eleusinian Mysteries evolved to be a profound celebration of the female experience of birth and motherhood, the loss of the innocence of childhood, separation from the mother over the issue of the daughter's developing sexuality (we should note here that in some versions of the myth, Persephone comes to love her husband and willingly accepts the division in her life), a symbolic experience of death and the underworld, re-union in maturity with the mother, an exploration of the spiritual that underlies and infuses all life, that brings all into balance and health. Women who successfully completed this spiritual journey were often considered "sibyls," possessors of wisdom valuable to the tribe. Primal stuff indeed, and a theme so powerful that we find echoes of it in later fairy tales, where the conflict often occurs between daughter and stepmother.

Perhaps the best example to begin this discussion of the female myth is Joan Vinge's *The Snow Queen* (1980), a novel that makes a good deal of conscious use of the Demeter/Persephone myth, to the point of naming a casino in Tiamat's capital city "Persiponë's Hell." Vinge reverses the connection between what we think of as the benevolence of the warm season when Persephone is with her mother Demeter with the cold sterility of the time when she is underground with Hades. Tiamat is a world with two stars orbiting a black hole in an extreme orbit, causing long years of winter, followed by long centuries of summer, each ruled by its own queen. The winter cycle is technologically advanced, thanks in great part to the tech-savvy visitors from the Hegemony who travel through a temporary gate offered by the black hole, but its scientific enlightenment is endangered once the cycle turns to the more agrarian summer, and the alien visitors leave, destroying all remnants of the planet's technology as they go. Arienrhod, Queen of Winter, hatches a plot to put a clone of herself on Summer's throne, thus saving the world from its cyclic plunge back into its own dark ages, and ensuring her legacy's survival through her clone.

However, things don't work out quite as planned. On her way to the capital city, the clone-daughter, Moon Dawntreader—unaware of her heritage—is abducted by "tech smugglers" and endures many revelations about the world she inhabits and her role in it. Some of these experiences off-world describe a harrowing visit to the darkness of the underworld:

> The limitless absence of light and life wrapped Moon's senses in a smothering shroud, deprived her of all sensations, Falling into a bottomless well, she knew herself for the last feeble spark of life in a universe where Death reigned undisputed…the consort of Death. (p. 136)

In the process, Moon discovers that she is a sibyl, the carrier of lost scientific and technological knowledge. She is driven on her quest in great part by her desire to re-unite with her childhood lover and cousin, Sparks. On re-encountering him, Moon reveals the wise woman she has become; she understands the devastation the departing offworlders cause:

> I began to see what you always saw, about progress, technology the—magic the offworlders do, and how it isn't magic to them. They understand so much more—they don't have to be afraid of disease, or broken bones, or childbirth…. We want knowledge, we're asking for our birthright. The offworlders want us to think it's wrong to be dissatisfied with what we have…. Change isn't evil– change is life. (p. 372)

The rivalry between mother and daughter erupts once Moon returns to Winter and discovers Sparks has become the lover of her mother, thus echoing a central theme of the Eleusinian mysteries: sexual rivalry between mother and daughter. The eventual reconciliation between the ambitions of mother and daughter—though not a happy one—promises a gifted and skillful queen to guide the world through its summer years.

Yet *The Snow Queen* is more than a science-fictional recasting of the myth of Demeter and Persephone. Vinge incorporates elements of other mythic themes, enriching the story with their subtext, the primary one being the story of the Snow Queen. Moon's cousin, Sparks, who falls under Arienrhod's spell, echoes the young men on the brink of adulthood who are seduced by the figure of the icy Snow Queen in both the Hans Christian Anderson tale and C. S. Lewis's novel published in 1950, *The Lion, The Witch and the Wardrobe* (note that "Dawntreader" points to a novel in Lewis's series). Further, Sparks overcomes the Queen's champion to become "Starbuck," whose ritual helmet employs a stag's antlers befitting the former champion's real name, Herne, a legendary hunter himself, often known as Orion, the huntsman in the sky. The hunt itself has dark underpinnings, for the hunted sea creatures—the Mers who carry a precious life-extending fluid in their veins—are sentient. (I'll return to the theme of the Great Hunt later.) The ending of the novel harkens back to other pre-historic rituals, in particular the sacrifice of the monarch at the end of the agricultural year in order to ensure that the land will flourish again under the successor:

> Moon raised her hands to the Sea, crying like a gull into the storm of the crowd's anticipation. "Lady Sea, Mother of us all, accept our gifts and return them ninefold, accept our sins and bring us renewal, accept the soul of Winter and let it be—reborn." She faltered imperceptibly. "Let Spring come to Summer!" (p. 394)

It isn't necessary that the reader consciously recognize any of these mythic or legendary echoes to enjoy this or any other story. They supply the emotional undercurrent that brings the reader to accept the inevitability of the sequence of events that make up Vinge's plot; we react to them because they are familiar to us on a deep level. Their use in a science fictional narrative, far from detracting from the scientific and technological background, only increases its power to move us.

Ursula Le Guin's story "Winter's King" (the first appearance, 1969, of material that she later developed fully in *The Left Hand of Darkness*) is also concerned with coldness and heat as symbols of different ways of life, or planets as is the case here. In this case, it is the Demeter figure who is "lost." Further complicating the original mythic material, Le Guin makes the inhabitants of Winter androgynous, their sex cyclic, and in this story the king, Argaven, is in a female cycle. The king discovers evidence of having been kidnaped and mind-altered by enemies, and makes the decision to abdicate in favor of the heir, Emran. Argaven leaves, seeking healing on an uncomfortably—for the king—warm world. Relativity being what it is, the king ages very little before returning to Winter, but the home-world's inhabitants have experienced the passage of sixty years, and Emran, old now, has become a tyrant needing to be deposed (another nod to the sickness of the world with Persephone absent). Yet far from finding a happy reconciliation here, we're told Emran commits suicide when Argaven returns. Le Guin stands the Greek myth on its head in many ways while remaining true to its inner wisdom; the major themes are still visible: mother/daughter estrangement, loss, reunion, wisdom gained at a price, and at the end, an almost Demeter-like moment of compassion for her lost daughter:

Stooping over the body, Argaven lifts up that cold hand and starts to take from the age-knotted forefingers the massive, carved gold ring. But she does not do it. "Keep it," she whispers, "keep it." For a moment she bends yet lower as if she whispered in the dead ear, or laid her cheek against the cold and wrinkled face. Then she straightens up and stands awhile and presently goes out through the dark corridors, by windows bright with distant ruin, to set her house in order: Argaven, Winter's King. (p. 113)

In Marge Piercy's influential feminist novel *Woman on the Edge of Time* (1976), the main character Consuelo Ramos (Connie) has been forcibly separated from her daughter Angelina by the authorities. Claiming that Connie is a sociopath, the authorities take her child to foster care and lock Connie in a mental institution (in many versions of the original myth, Demeter is considered mad for her extreme grief). The two versions of the future that Connie is transported to while still incarcerated may or may not be hallucinations, but in any case they are as bleak and unattractive as the world without Persephone, and in one case, sterile as women no longer bear children. Another notable feminist work is Joanna Russ's *The Female Man* (1975), which also touches on the Eleusinian themes of mother/daughter relationships, loss of contact, and eventual reunion and enlightenment, while at the same time producing a text that is sometimes brutally disapproving of current male/female relationships.

A thought-provoking take on the gulf in understanding between male and female experience appears in a story by Alice Sheldon, who published under the pseudonym James Tiptree Jr, "The Women Men Don't

See" (1973). The men in the story, including the narrator, Don, are down in the Yucatan on a fishing trip, an Odyssean-type undertaking; when their little plane crashes in the jungle they adopt another script from the Hero's Journey: the search for a way out. The behavior of the women, a mother and daughter puzzles Don. The mother, Mrs Parsons rejects all his comforting talk about the important role women play in a society he has to admit is run by men. The story gives us an unflattering picture of society lacking the feminine influence (a world where Demeter is deprived of Persephone's presence): a world of drugs, violence, cynical politics. Then an almost unbelievable encounter with visiting aliens occurs, and Don is confronted with a very different level of the female experience. Once he realizes Mrs Parsons and her daughter are hoping to be abducted by the extraterrestrials, he comments, "She's as alien as they are." Perhaps Persephone, returning from the Underworld, would have seemed equally as alien.

In place of adventure and physical action, Demeter stories often make abundant use of symbolic or metaphoric imagery. One story, I think, sets the standard: Pamela Zoline's "The Heat Death of the Universe" (1967), an unrelenting catalog of trivial items and seemingly meaningless actions in the day of a young mother experiencing a nervous breakdown that nevertheless add up to a profound revelation of the nature of Demeter's experience. (Compare this to Tim O'Brien's Vietnam novel, *The Things They Carried* (1990), which makes use of the same device.)

As a side-note, I offer the interesting comparison that feminist critic Sandra M. Gilbert makes (1983) between Persephone and the character of Ayesha, She-Who-Must-be-Obeyed in H. Rider Haggard's 1887 novel, *She*. "An interesting cross between Venus and Persephone…

as Persephone She is married to Death and queen in a country of shadows. Shrouded in a 'white and gauzy material' that makes her look like a 'corpse in its grave clothes' She judges and condemns" (p. 127).

An outcome of wisdom gained needs to be mentioned if briefly, and that is the third figure who emerges in the myth of the Maiden and the Mother: the Crone, sometimes known as Hecate. With age comes wisdom, the sibyl that Moon Dawntreader becomes as a result of her journey into the "underworld," but we also recognize the power for wildness and mischief that the crone represents. Women's "magic" was scary to the ancient Greeks; they gave us a parade of nasty females like Medusa and Medea. In sf today, we're more likely to find the archetype of the "Wise Woman" who uses intuition and cosmic connection along with the more traditionally male pursuits of science and technology. Isaac Asimov's Dr Susan Calvin, chief robopsychologist in the Robot series, is an example. And it's interesting to note that the Bene Gesserit of Frank Herbert's *Dune* (1965) starts out as an esteemed order of wise women and ends up being considered a group of witches by the very person their knowledge of genetics bred into being: Paul Atreiedes.

Heinlein would probably classify these Demeter/Persephone stories as having "[Wo]man who learns better" plots. What these protagonists seek to learn is the answer to the great questions: What makes us human? What is the meaning of life? Writing about this is not limited to female authors. The subtext of Demeter's story is the crucial nature of this inner side of our shared human experience. In *Women Who Run with the Wolves* (1992), the Jungian psychologist, Clarissa Pinkola Estés writes:

It is not by accident that the pristine wilderness of our planet disappears as the understanding of our own inner wild nature fades. It is also not difficult to comprehend why old forests and old women are viewed as not very important resources…. It is not so coincidental that wolves and coyotes, bears and wildish women have similar reputations. They all share related, instinctual archetypes. (p. 1)

A message of such timeless importance finds its place in stories about the future. Much of the literature of science fiction acts like Albert Einstein's *gedankenexperimenten,* a special laboratory of the mind where unthinkable events can be contemplated and discarded before they harm us. Both paths, Odysseus's outward journey and Demeter's way inside, are part of human experience, as vital to us today as they were to our ancestors.

Playing God

When Mary Shelley came to choose the title for her most famous novel, *Frankenstein* (1818), she added a subtitle, *The Modern Prometheus,* thus identifying her story with one of the two most important of the ancient myths for our scientific age, and certainly for science fiction (the other is the Hero's Journey). In Greek mythology, Prometheus was one of the Elder Race, the Titans, who were later supplanted by Zeus and his pantheon of gods. It was Prometheus—in some versions of the myth, the creator of humans—who climbed Olympus, stole fire from the chariot of the sun, and gave it to poor, shivering humanity. As a result, humans learned to fend off predatory animals who shared their world, to shelter themselves from inclement climates, to cook food that was otherwise inedible, and to develop tools both benign and warlike. Thus the whole endeavor we know as science eventually came to dominate the world to the point where humans would repudiate the gods themselves. For this awesome and ultimately dangerously subversive act, Zeus punished Prometheus by chaining him on Mount Caucasus where vultures preyed on his liver every night. Since Prometheus was one of the immortals, the liver regrew the next day. Severe punishment indeed! Obviously the Greeks felt it fitted a crime of such magnitude, for fire both set humans free of the gods and made them gods in themselves, a double-edged sword of a gift.

Mordecai Roshwald suggests in *Dreams and Nightmares* (2008) that there are two other candidates for mythic benefactor of the human race. The first of these is Daedalus, the ingenious proto-engineer who created the labyrinth for Minos's monster amongst other things, and the wings that were to free himself and his son Icarus from captivity, and second, Noah, responsible not only for building the ark that saved humanity from the flood, but also the founder of agriculture, planting a vineyard and tilling the ground for crops. Daedalus paid the price for hubris through the death of his son, for obviously the power of flight belongs to the gods. But Noah lived to a ripe old age, unscathed—unless we consider that one of his sons murdered the other.

To us in a scientific age where we increasingly possess the power to create and destroy ourselves, the myth is obviously a metaphoric warning about the danger of playing god. Fire represents the light of Knowledge, and indeed of Science, whose gifts can be both blessing and curse, sometimes both at once. But I think its message goes deeper than the warning that tools can both help and harm. However advanced humanity's knowledge may become, the myth suggests, we may never be able to live up to the role of wise gods of our own destiny.

In earlier periods of history, there was the notion that there are some things humankind should not be allowed to know—or do—a recognition of the limits of our ethical or moral judgment, or at least of our shaky ability to reign in our destructive desires. Today, Prometheus the Immortal has become the figure of the scientist, all too mortal. Yet even in the Middle Ages, the central point of the story of Prometheus's dangerous gift had emerged as the cautionary tale of Doctor Faustus, whose downfall was his desire to usurp God's power to control the creation of life by resurrecting the dead because he'd fallen in lust with the idea of the beautiful Helen of Troy. Faustus was an alchemist, practitioner of a mystical, semi-magical field of endeavor that eventually led to the development of science. But the importance of this version of the Prometheus story is that it doesn't fault him for his attempts to distill gold out of base metal, only for aspiring to a power that, once-possessed by a flawed mortal, would upset the very fabric of life.

Yet it is in one of science fiction's earliest works, Shelley's *Frankenstein,* that we find, perhaps for the first time, emphasis placed on the theme of the responsibility of the scientist for the results brought about by his or her creations, no matter how well-intentioned they may be. Creating life and restoring it from the dead are two powers considered to be godlike; to claim either one of them entails godlike responsibility. Like Faustus before him, Frankenstein challenged the gods head-on with his scientific work. We should ignore the various Hollywood treatments of this story, because they warp the theme, frequently turning it into a tale of mindless horror, whereas Shelley had a larger point to make. Victor Frankenstein, clearly sees himself as playing God:

> Life and death appeared to me ideal bounds, which I should first break through and pour a torrent of light into our dark world. A new species would bless me as its creator and source; many happy and excellent natures would owe their being to me. (p. 55)

Unfortunately, Frankenstein doesn't accept the responsibility that goes along with such power. Horrified by what he has created once he gets a good look at it, he abandons his creation—not just once, at its "birth," but also a second time when he refuses the monster's entreaty to create an Eve for this new Adam. Condemned by its creator to a lonely and loveless life of persecution, the monster makes his complaint:

> Oh Frankenstein…. Remember that I am thy creature; I ought to be thy Adam, but I am rather the fallen angel, whom thou drivest from joy for no misdeed. Everywhere I see bliss, from which I alone am irrevocably excluded. I was benevolent and good; misery made me a fiend. (p. 90)

And so, to Frankenstein's chagrin, the monster goes rampaging through his world. As the Greeks knew, even the gods must accept responsibility for the results of their creations. Frankenstein, like Prometheus, suffers greatly as a result of his work.

In *The Island of Doctor Moreau* (1896), H. G. Wells gives us another scientist obsessed with the goal of creating a new race of humans, although Doctor Moreau begins not with dead bodies but live animals. His hubris is no less than Frankenstein's. "To this day," he tells his incredulous shipwrecked visitor, Prendick, "I have never troubled about the ethics of the matter. The study of Nature makes a man at last as remorseless as Nature" (p. 225). Perhaps Moreau has lofty goals in mind, not the least being of some benefit to the uplifted creatures, but my experience has been that the gift of Prometheus has brought much pain as well as profit. The study of nature and the natural world is the realm of science, but perhaps the scientist cannot avoid the question of the ethics of what he or she—or others—does with this knowledge. To act otherwise is to invite disaster.

Characters who were scientists in stories written before 1945 either benefitted humanity or, like Frankenstein and Moreau—though quite unethical—caused damage on a personal or limited scale. Pulp science fiction was filled with engineer types, inventors, garage tinkerers, all of them capable of cobbling together fantastic solutions to the problems facing society; ethical concerns were ignored or downplayed. Not surprisingly, the fiction mirrored the enterprising character of its time, where the news of the day was filled with stories about the Wright Brothers, the Edisons, the Watts, the Fords, the Marie Curies who were making life so much better and brighter. It was a period when Prometheus had just come down the mountain with his fiery brand, lighting the cold, dark night for a grateful humanity. The bloodthirsty wolves of disease and poverty were retreating, and the food tasted better every day. This aspect of the myth of Prometheus gave rise to a lot of stories that we today regard as simplistic or shallow.

But even then, some writers sensed a troublesome future looming. Theodore Sturgeon's novelette "Microcosmic God" (1941) gives us a protagonist, Kidder, who creates a race of very small beings he names "neoterics." Since their life span is very short, he is able to progress them through many generations of evolution, exploring his own ideas. The novelette ends with the real threat that these constructs could take over the world. The echo of Frankenstein is loud here: becoming like gods carries its own danger.

After the atomic bomb was used on Hiroshima and Nagasaki in 1945, there was a profound shift in the mood of science fiction stories featuring scientists at work. There was no longer a way for writers or their readers to ignore the terrifying effects of this most modern use of fire. As a result, science fiction became absorbed in studying the global consequences of the scientists' studies and in the growing realization that we had become capable of doing ourselves irreparable damage before we'd developed the wisdom to avoid it. In another Sturgeon story, "Memorial" (1946), Doctor Grenfell, a scientist who once worked at Los Alamos, dreams of creating a nuclear event, a memorial so horrifying that its devastating aftermath will finally scare humanity into lasting peace. But the story also suggests that the solution may cause its own problems. "Judgment Day" (1955), by L. Sprague de Camp, introduces an atomic scientist smarting over childhood injuries, who decides to take revenge by making public a discovery that he hopes will result in the destruction of Earth, a definite illustration of the knowledge-without-wisdom problem! And Walter Miller's *A Canticle for Leibowitz* (1960) presents a cold-natured natural scientist, Thon Taddeo, considering the scraps of scientific information that desert monks in the monastery of St. Leibowitz have patiently saved and copied over the centuries after a nuclear disaster has destroyed civilization, leaving a tattered but not cowed Catholic Church to painstakingly pick up the pieces. Taddeus knows full well this knowledge once led to devastation and human annihilation; nevertheless he dreams of recreating the dangerous technology. The novel ends with the very real possibility that it will all happen again. Once humanity has accepted the flaming torch from Prometheus, we see that there is little desire to give it back.

Nuclear disaster wasn't the only boogeyman to inhabit the pages of science fiction after 1945. Kurt Vonnegut takes another tack in *Cat's Cradle* (1963). Here, the scientist, Doctor Felix Hoenneker, creates a substance dubbed "Ice Nine" that is so powerful the smallest sliver will cause an ocean to freeze over permanently. Hoenneker joins the ranks of characters representing the amorality of science blinded by hubris; even knowing the horror his discovery is capable of, should it escape from his control, he continues with its development in the name of science. Vonnegut clearly doesn't accept the convenient separation of "theoretical" and "practical" science when blame has to be assigned; obviously, he was influenced by the trauma suffered by many in the scientific community when the theoretical work of splitting the atom became the practical destruction of Hiroshima. And while the protagonist of George R.R. Martin's novelette "The Sand Kings" (1979) isn't a scientist, he conducts godlike experiments on his captive alien colonies with horrifying results. Like these stories, an illustration of all the Promethean cautionary tales is Michael Crichton's *Jurassic Park* (1990). John Hammond, the billionaire founder and CEO of International Genetic Technologies, has usurped a godlike power to create life by reviving several dinosaur species for entertainment and/or educational values in a theme park, an enterprise that has disastrous results.

The Windup Girl, by Paolo Bacigalupi (2009), goes further in its indictment of out-of-control modern Prometheus. Set in an over-populated India, Bacigalupi puts a bio-engineering company, Agri-Gen, on the spot for the havoc it causes through crop engineering in an attempt to control the world's harvests, and the bio-terrorism that inevitably occurs in the process. Like the gift of Prometheus to shivering humans, Agri-Gen's bio-engineered food promises sustenance and prosperity to the starving masses of the world. But it carries the seeds of a dangerous dependency with it, the destruction of sources of natural crops, and ultimately the economic enslavement of the world.

These post-1945 stories are dystopic nightmares, their message clear: it's dangerous for humans to usurp godlike powers without possessing the corresponding godlike wisdom. This is not an indictment of scientists or scientific advance per se, only a warning about the need to consider motive and long-term effect. Science is based on the idea that the universe's laws are logical and can be understood and put to the advantage of humanity; science fiction writers attempt to chart that progress, envisioning the utopia that can result if all goes well, or the dystopia if it does not. The motivation of the scientist/protagonist in these works echoes the underlying myth of Prometheus. Most of these characters have Prometheus's goal in mind; they are sincerely working to bring what they see as a boon to humanity. But one of two things happens; they either overlook the reality that humans can use the most positive boon in the most negative way, that fire can burn as well as light the path, or the scientists themselves are corrupted by the power they wield.

It would be unthinkable to close a section on characters "playing God" without referring to the single largest collection of such imposters all in one novel. I'm referring, of course, to Roger Zelazny's celebrated novel *Lord of Light* (1967), where the crew of a starship (named, in case we miss the point, *Star of India*) finds that the way to survival is to adopt the identities of the Hindu pantheon of gods and use their advanced technology (here called Aspects) in ancient ways to control the hapless passengers. Staying close to Hindu theology, Zelazny gives us an absorbing, sometimes hilariously funny, view of the way this works out over centuries; the crew also have access to a machine that can transfer minds between bodies, thus "reincarnation" and the wheel of reward and punishment in the next life are in place. Determined to upset this scenario, we find Mahasamatman, or Great-Souled Sam (but he prefers to be called "Sam"), one of the original colonists who singlehandedly fights to bring Buddhism into the picture. Zelazny has used the world's mythologies several times in novels about present-day characters, but this one is probably his best.

While we don't give much credence today to the old idea that there are some things humans must not know, some areas we should not meddle with, we do still see the value in the ancient myth of Prometheus. The theme of today's science fiction seems to be that if we don't want to invite Zeus's terrible retribution, we must exercise caution when playing with our wonderful new toys.

The Goddess and the Geoscientists

The ten-foot-tall blue natives in the movie *Avatar* (2009) plug the tips of their braids into the flora and fauna of their world for communication, and the human invaders realize that the entire planet Pandora is a living entity, a closed system. Before James Cameron's film, Disney's *The Lion King* (1994) preached the circle of life, but neither Cameron nor Disney invented the concept.

Three thousand years ago, the Natural Philosophy espoused by the Greeks taught that the world is a living creature, Gaia, the Neolithic Mother Goddess, oldest of divinities, from which all things spring, and in which all things are connected. In some accounts, the female trinity of Demeter (mother), Persephone (virgin), and Hecate (crone) are aspects of Gaia, and Aphrodite, goddess of love, is Gaia's daughter. This notion of the interconnectedness of life was not confined to the Greeks. Early societies, particularly matrilineal ones, taught that Earth is our mother, and like a mother it nurtures us and is affected by our actions. Some went even further and taught that all parts of the universe are capable of influencing each other. Buddhism, too, speaks of our deep connection to our planet; in the words of Zen Master Dogen, "You and the streams and the mountains are one and the same." And in 1854, Chief Seattle said, "All things are bound together. All things connect." In European folklore, many medieval tales are versions of the myth of the dying land ruled by a wounded king; the fate of the ruler and his kingdom are connected, so the healing of the one will become the return to health of the other (which is related to the Greek belief that Demeter mourns for Persephone in the underworld, and the Earth is therefore not allowed to bloom and fruit until she returns). In these stories, a Hero figure, usually a knight in armor, undertakes a quest to find some version of the Holy Grail, which will bring healing to the king, and thus to the land he rules. We might even go so far as to say that the ailing king is a metaphor for human consciousness in its relationship to the sick and endangered planet. We'll return to that idea later.

Remnants of this world view can be found in the entertainment section of the daily newspaper, in the pronouncements of astrology where the perceived conjunction of planets is assumed to affect human destiny. But in the western world it went out of style with the advent of Judeo-Christianity and the belief that the world and its inhabitants were created to be a hierarchy with Man at the top. Closer to our time, we find Darwin's theory of how things evolved, which evokes the theory of survival of the fittest, not exactly an archetype of connection and cooperation. Not much interrelation there, other than the kind that says if the nutritious leaves are up high, herbivores like giraffes will grow longer necks to reach them. In fact, neo-Darwinian evolutionary biologists were the ones most opposed to the idea of interconnection when it re-emerged and was first presented to the scientific community in the twentieth century.

Scientific viewpoints began to shift in the 1970s, along with the emerging cultural-environmental views of the era, away from separation toward cooperation. Two scientists in particular were responsible for the new paradigm, James Lovelock, a chemist, and Lynn Margulis, a biologist; they became the godparents of the new science of Gaia with their groundbreaking hypothesis of the Earth as a closed, self-regulating system (1985). Life, they proposed, had a regulatory impact on Earth's geochemical cycles and climate, favoring organisms and living processes. Some theoretical scientists were willing to go even farther than that already revolutionary view, in support of the "strong" version of the Gaia hypothesis that the Earth itself is alive, speculating that humans have evolved to be the consciousness of the whole. This is perhaps related to or a natural progression from the thought experiment of Schrödinger's cat, which showed us that in the quantum world, things seem not to happen until the observer enters the equation. In 2001, a joint conference of several different branches of Earth sciences meeting in Amsterdam summed up the middle ground. The Earth, the conference decided, behaved as a self-regulating system composed of physical, chemical, biological, and human components. Since then, there's been an explosion of scientific research into areas such as the co-evolution of life and the environment, thermodynamics and the purpose of life, the importance of even the least species to the health of the biosphere as a whole, and a recognition of shared DNA between humans and animals and plant life. An astounding recent report (2009) even postulated that minerals, including some semi-precious stones, have evolved from the primitive Earth along with—and because of—life itself. Sometimes, the scholarly papers in this emerging field of science read like science fiction!

So let's consider whether the genre has kept up with the science or been ahead of the curve as we might hope. Even before the geoscientists had clarified their thinking on just how far the inter-connectedness of all Earth's systems might extend, sf authors were already exploring the possibilities. Examples of living worlds, such as Murray Leinster's short story "The Lonely Planet" (1949) and Ursula K. Le Guin's "Vaster than Empires and More Slow" (1975), were published long before the Amsterdam conference agreed on the more conservative, so-called "weak hypothesis" of active feed-back mechanisms operating on the planet as a whole. In Le Guin's story, the Hainish biologist, Harfer, one of the team of scientists sent to investigate worlds that had not been seeded or settled by the founding race of Hain, reports on his discovery, "[The root nodes] are all interconnected, both by the root-node linkage and by your green epiphytes in the branches. A linkage of incredible and physical extent." And Osden, his fellow explorer, agrees:

> Sentience without senses. Blind, deaf, nerveless, moveless. Some irritability, response to touch. Response to sun, to light, to water, and chemicals in the earth around the roots. Nothing comprehensible to an animal mind. Presence without mind. Awareness of being, without object or subject. Nirvana. (p. 517)

Other authors were extending the idea of living worlds to stars and nebulae; for example, Frank Herbert's *Whipping Star* (1970), Fred Hoyle's short novel *The Black Cloud* (1957), and Gregory Benford and Gordon Ecklund's *If the Stars Are Gods* (1977), all of which appeared before the geoscientists held their conference.

One of the most interesting conceptions of a planetary consciousness occurs in Stanislaw Lem's *Solaris* (1961), an intelligent planetary ocean, one of the best portraits of an "inscrutable alien" in science fiction, becomes the antagonist in the novel, acting upon the human explorers and reacting to them, driving the action. (The novel has been filmed twice; both versions are unfortunately unmemorable.) And maybe the strangest version of the Gaia hypothesis occurs in David Brin's novel *Earth* (1990), which is filled with eco-collapse, black holes, artificial intelligence and—perhaps—a form of an emerging planetary mind.

Once again, as we've come to expect, science fiction outpaces science in offering explanations about our world. But what explains the layman's interest in the hypothesis that the Earth is a living entity, a belief that predates scientific exploration by several thousand years? Lucky guess? Superstition? Labeling it superstition is not the same as explaining it, for superstitions often betray remnants of older religious beliefs where all has vanished except a lingering trace of the numinous once associated with great mysteries. Or do we carry a gene that programs us to look for the presence of the spiritual— or "God"—in the very foundation of our world? Could it be that the mystics had it right? Recently (January 27, 2010), a scientific article in the *New York Times* asked, "Is There an Ecological Unconscious?" Apparently, such concepts are no longer only the stuff of science fiction or arcane mystical exploration. If the world is indeed a living entity and we are part of it, learning separation as we grow out of childhood, then it would come as no surprise that we should harbor vestigial traces, unconscious memories, of that unity.

But perhaps there is no conflict between the myth of Mother Gaia and the geoscientists who would explain Her in modern terms. In other words, what happens if we accept the ancient story as metaphor? If we can answer that in the affirmative, maybe there's hope for us. It may turn out that for us in the present the most important myth we should re-examine is the one about the wounded king and the dying world around him, recognizing that the king may represent our own inner spiritual being in need of healing before we destroy the "kingdom" of our planet, either through the devastations of war or through ecological collapse.

Clowns, Dead Dogs, and the Universe

If we'd been alive in Syria sometime in the sixth century CE, we might have witnessed a peculiar sight. A man dressed in rags, who has recently been living in the desert, is dragging the body of a dead dog through the streets and into the church. What's going on? That was just the beginning of the strange and unsettling tricks that Abba Simeon used to lure people to God. Saint Simeon, as he later became, is the first recorded Holy Fool of the western world, and—not surprisingly—the patron saint of clowns to this day. There was a purpose to Simeon's mad behavior; such foolish-seeming antics drew people's attention, defused their skepticism, and allowed the gospel message to permeate their hearts and minds.

Simeon is the first of what became a long line of Holy Fools or Holy Innocents in history and literature, characters so simple and silly that we perceive an innocence about them, perhaps even the aura of holiness. (The root form of the adjective "silly" is the Old English *saelig*, soulful, or blessed. By Shakespeare's time the word's meaning had slipped to "weak" or "simple.") The true role of characters like the Holy Fool, or the Sacred Clowns of Hopi tradition, is to get past our intellectual defenses through laughter, allowing us to perceive the world around us and our place in it in a different way. At the very least, the Fool hopes to break our deadly cynicism that prevents us from seeing what's staring us in the face. Throughout the ancient European world, the jester in attendance at the royal court was often the only one allowed to criticize their majesties and get away with it, such criticism to be veiled in foolish-seeming speech and antics. In due time we have literary examples of the wisdom of the Holy Fool: Gimpel the Fool, Mullah Nasruddin, Don Quixote, Parsifal, and later, Forrest Gump. Today, some of the most biting social criticism comes from comedians on tv shows such as *Saturday Night Live*. But the Fool's roots go even deeper than that, into mythology in the case of the Norse god Loki, where benevolent innocence gives way to a more malevolent intent, but the end result is the same: encountering this archetypal figure, we're forced out of our comfort zones and made to contemplate the truth of existence.

There is another aspect to the Fool's character, one that has roots in mystic tradition, and that is the one that appears on the Tarot cards. The Fool, numbered zero in the Major Arcana, shows the figure of a rather preoccupied young man about to step off a cliff, with a dog snapping at his heels while butterflies circle his head. This presents one of the most puzzling images in the deck of strange pictures, and it's easy to dismiss the entire deck as superstitious belief or outright nonsense. After all, we have a tradition of gypsy fortune tellers reading the future of gullible clients from these cards in exchange for money. (The other deck, known as the Minor Arcana, gave rise to the Clubs, Spades, Hearts and Diamonds of today's playing cards.) But it was Jung's belief that the Major Arcana, carried ancient, often mystical teachings about the meaning of life that needed to be disguised in a time of persecution from the

Roman Catholic church. The Fool's butterflies are the key to this image; metamorphosing from a lowly crawling caterpillar to a gorgeous winged creature, they represent the stages of growth of the human soul. As we've seen, myths are much concerned with spiritual growth and evolution, and in this aspect, the Fool speaks to the human soul.

When we look at the characters in any work of fiction, genre or mainstream, we notice that some types appear over and over; we call them "stock characters," which implies they are all relatively predictable. Not surprisingly, science fiction has its share of characters that seem sent over from Central Casting for the occasion. Perhaps we can clarify the distinction by looking at what the Holy Fool is *not*. The most obvious, related stock character we meet in this genre is the Naive Observer, the person along on the adventure who is mostly clueless, thus allowing the rest of the characters to explain things to him. This nicely avoids the problem of characters having to hold up the galactic war to say to each other, "As you know, Bob…" in order to get vital information to the reader. Another such character is the Outsider, the non-engineer, civilian-in-army-territory, hick-from-the-hills finding himself or herself in the city—all of them apparently capable of seeing the problem with fresh eyes and proposing a workable solution that the experts couldn't imagine. This character is particularly beloved in American genre fiction, the inventor/tinkerer who comes up with the gadget that saves the world when the highly educated scientists and highly trained engineers have given up; Robert Heinlein in particular liked to use such characters.

Sometimes this character appears as a Trickster, another form of the archetype. The Loarra in Terry Carr's "The Dance of the Changer and the Three" (1968) take this transformation one step further, becoming the "inscrutable alien":

> I discovered that it didn't matter much just who I was talking with: none of them made any more sense than the others. They were all, as far as I was and am concerned, totally crazy, incomprehensible, stupid, silly, and plain damn no good. (p. 180)

Carr's aliens can be welcoming or murderous by turn; humans are the recipients of their unwelcome and little understood activities.

Roger Zelazny's character Sam, in *Lord of Light*, can be considered a Trickster, and a recent version appears in Adam Roberts' *Jack Glass* (2012), where Glass, an enigmatic, unsentimental figure assumes various personalities to confuse and manipulate those who have dealings with him; Glass is no Fool, holy or otherwise; he pursues his own devious plans across the solar system.

None of these characters, no matter how clumsy, ignorant, or boorish, rises to the level of the Holy Fool unless other qualities such as genuine innocence are present. The Holy Fool is part naive observer, part pure innocent. When the roots of a stock character are particularly ancient, and our response to this character borders on the numinous, we are dealing with an archetype, defined by Jung in *Psychology and Religion* (1953) as images that occur all over the earth as constituents of myth and also as individual products of unconscious origin. The Mother Goddess is one such archetype; the Holy Fool is another.

One of the most memorable Holy Fools in science fiction is Brother Francis Gerard in Walter Miller's *A Canticle for Leibowitz*, mentioned previously for its use of the Prometheus figure. Six centuries after a devastating nuclear war, the bumbling but innocent novice Brother Francis is scavenging in some ruins when he comes across a few relics of his order's founder, including what Brother Francis believes are the founder's scriptures. We readers soon figure out that the "Blessed Leibowitz" was in actuality one of the nuclear scientists responsible for the catastrophe, and these holy scriptures Brother Francis reveres are circuit diagrams and shopping lists. Yet the monk's innocent actions ultimately lead to Leibowitz being canonized. While we're laughing at the "foolish" mistake of believing scraps of engineering diagrams or shopping lists are worthy of veneration, we learn that they contain valuable information for the monks who are trying to rebuild civilization, one invention at a time. Brother Francis's actions lead to the consequence that twelve hundred years later, the whole cycle of nuclear threat and disaster will be repeated. Thus the Fool's message to us here is one of warning. (We might also note that this novel contains yet another archetypal character, the Wandering Jew, who witnesses all the centuries of folly and comments on it too.)

Sometimes, the plot of a story provides the central characters, the starship captains and the chief scientists, with a problem that evades their ability to figure it out. Perhaps they're trying too hard, or maybe they're not good at thinking outside the box. The author could just step in and hand the protagonist a clue: "Look, people! I just found the Rosetta Stone that explains everything." But where's the fun in that? Besides, it's not believable and denies the reader the pleasure of figuring things out along with the characters. Here's where the Holy Fool is useful, asking the questions no one else bothers to ask, stumbling toward the solution denied to those with more expertise.

This character is also more than just the Outsider figure Heinlein utilized, for the Outsider lacks influence, not smarts. Allowed to tinker with the problem, the Outsider comes up with a solution that leaves others wondering why they didn't think of it. Often, the Outsider is also the Hero of the story in the Odyssean sense, though he may not have started out that way. And the Fool isn't the same as the dummy who messes things up and complicates the plot—sometimes for malevolent reasons, thus becoming the antagonist. The significant thing about the Holy Fool, when we suspect we've found one in a story, is his or her purity of motive and innocence of action; the Holy Fool stands outside of conventional thinking and has no hidden personal agenda. He or she asks questions the other, more knowledgeable characters consider beside the point, off-topic, valueless, childish, easily dismissed as not fitting "received wisdom" or at times science itself. The category includes Davy, the poorly-educated ward of the state in the apocalyptic world of Edgar Pangborn's novel (1964) of the same name, and to a certain extent, Valentine Michael Smith from Robert Heinlein's *Stranger in a Strange Land* (1961). Mars-raised Smith is the ultimate innocent, a naive, well-meaning young man whose profound message of tolerance is little understood and ultimately rejected by Earth-raised humans.

The Fool's behavior, dragging that dead dog across the planet, alternately puzzles and irritates the rest of the characters, often unsettling them when they're trying hardest to figure things out. And that's the whole point. Whether the Fool is a holy idiot or crazy as a fox like Simeon or the Hopi Clowns, his or her job is to break through the stereotypical thinking the others are indulging in. Or that the reader is caught up in. For sometimes the main characters of the story just won't get it, but the reader is left wondering if the Fool wasn't right after all. Another, more cynical way of saying this is to suggest that the author is having her cake and eating it too, scrupulously following scientific reason on the one hand, and cracking open the story for doubt, mysticism, and all manner of strangeness to creep in on the other.

Often the writer doesn't know beforehand that's what the Fool is going to do—often doesn't even know ahead of time the character is a Holy Fool. Characters have a way of birthing themselves in a writer's head and running away with the best planned plots. Sorel Varney was only meant to be a retarded "handyjack," (handyman, jack-of-all-trades) a minor character along on the mission to take care of chores while the others explored the planet, when I started to write the lingster story "Stranger Than Imagination Can" (2007). By the end of the story I was convinced that as a result of his innocence, his love of the work the lingsters did, and his magical thinking, he instinctively understood more about the aliens who once inhabited the planet than any of the smarter characters. Naturally, he couldn't convincingly explain any of it to the others, but I hope the reader will think about the possibilities he's raised:

> If only he could prove to Petra the beings were still here, because of course they were.... He heard them singing everywhere in the white city, and sometimes he caught glimpses of something out of the corner of his eye just as he entered a street or passed a wall. The others didn't seem to see or hear anything, but that didn't make it any less real. (p. 140)

As the scientist J. B. S. Haldane famously said in 1927, "The universe is not only queerer than we imagine, it's queerer than we can imagine." I suspect that the more we learn about the universe and our place in it, the more we'll realize there are any number of things we can't understand. Abba Simeon's converts might never have been able to explain the doctrine of the Holy Trinity, but the saint made certain they experienced its numinosity. Maybe it always takes a Holy Fool to make sure we experience even when we don't understand.

The Magi's Starship

On January 6th, the western Christian church celebrates the visit of three kings bearing symbolic gifts to a newborn child in Judea. Sometimes called "Wise Men" or "Magi," these shadowy figures were probably astrologers (synonymous with astronomers in those early days before the birth of modern science) since they were following the appearance of a new star that might have been a comet—or, as Arthur C. Clarke speculated in his classic short story "The Star" (1955), a supernova that incinerated its own planetary system. That's all we know about them; we don't know how many of them there were (three is a symbolic number), and their names are a later addition to the tale. Although the Gospel of Matthew tells us they came from the "east" and traveled "west," this may be due to the fact that the east (Persia, home of Zoroastrianism) was reputed to be the source of both learning and sorcery at the time. This is sufficiently heady stuff that it has continued to fire the human imagination down the centuries.

We've long been fascinated by the magician archetype in literature, a fascination that stretches in western civilization from Merlin to Prospero to Gandalf to Albus Dumbledore. Even earlier, tribes had their shamans, and Greeks and Egyptians had their priests who could speak for the gods and call down the supernatural powers. We want to believe there are some humans, like us but not entirely so, who can escape the laws of nature that bind the rest of us, bending them to their will. We fantasize about the mysterious few who stand with one foot in our everyday reality and the other in a realm we can never reach. Sometimes that achievement comes with a terrible price, and our folklore gives us Doctor Faustus who sold his soul to the devil for love of Helen of Troy, or Doctor Parnassus in Terry Gilliam's movie *The Imaginarium of Dr Parnassus* (2009), where the eponymous protagonist possesses a magic mirror courtesy of his own "deal with the devil." There is considerable overlap between the magus, the wizard, and the alchemist, one of the most famous of the latter being Queen Elizabeth I's John Dee, who appears as a character in John Crowley's *Aegypt* (1987). Alchemists were proto-scientists, experimenting with the effects of combining different substances and elements, but all three have, in their turn, enthralled our ancestors. Wizards, magi, and alchemists are not to be confused with the conjuror whose skills are seen to be entirely of this world, fit to entertain and mystify children and the common folk with card tricks but little else.

If we have any doubt about the continuing fascination of this concept, we have only to examine the present-day popularity of stage magicians. Some, like David Copperfield or Penn and Teller on stage in Las Vegas, may intimate that making the elephant disappear is magic, but in our scientific age we know it's a clever, well-rehearsed trick. We enjoy the effects, but as adults we aren't fooled into belief. Occasionally, a magician comes along like the late Doug Henning, a follower of the eastern sage Maharishi Mahesh Yogi whose disciples practiced levitation. Henning turned the tables on this stage-magician patter and earnestly confided that though his tricks might look like magic, they were really just tricks. The more Henning protested the effects were tricks, the more our inner child suspected they were magic and that Henning was a genuine Magus. Another of Henning's influences, Houdini, seems well on the way to assuming the reputation of Magus himself. We experience more than just entertainment witnessing these "magical" acts, occasionally amounting to a shiver of strangeness that indicates the presence of the numinous. The fact that we understand we are being tricked but are neither enraged nor disappointed bears witness to the continuing power of this archetype.

Neil Burger, writer and director of the movie *The Illusionist* (2006), spoke of the appeal of "[T]he uncanny sense that nothing is what it seems…the idea of coming face to face with something unexplainable." In other words, a conjuror who fools us with ingenious tricks remains just a talented stage performer, and one whose marvelous effects (miracles) are attributed to a deity might be a saint, but that's not the power of the Magus. We might note here that the three kings didn't claim to have received word from God at the start of their journey; they were simply following the apparent path of a star. The conjuror is just an entertainer, the saint out of our reach, but the Magus compels.

In mainstream literature, John Fowles' *The Magus* (1966) and Peter Straub's *Shadowland* (1980) provide two examples of this trope. Not surprisingly, the fantasy genre is filled with images of the figure that transcends—or appears to—our reality; some are great wizards like Merlin and Gandalf, some petty conjurors, all of them performing supernatural tricks, a few rising to the more exalted status of Magus. The difference, not trivial in terms of effect on the reader's enjoyment of the story, is that in work like Fowles's, the strange effects the Magus creates aren't explained by the laws of science, nor are we asked to believe they are miracles. In this, the authors seem to follow the example of Matthew: Here's the story; take it or leave it.

What about science fiction? Surely a genre that is based on the underlying reality of the physical laws of nature can't allow itself such a wildly improbable figure as the Magus? But a character that doesn't base claims to performing marvels on divine authority is little threat to the reader's scientific sensibilities. We assume that there are laws of behavior in the physical universe that we haven't yet/may not ever discover let alone control. How oddly comforting to our trembling inner child at the edge of the Void, from which the gods have apparently been banished, that *somebody* is still in charge! Given the persistence of the Magus archetype, we can assume it arises in response to something deep in the human psyche. If this is true, examples should continue to occur even in hard sf in the future.

The problem is, as Arthur C. Clarke put it succinctly for us, any sufficiently advanced technology will be indistinguishable from magic. For an example of this, imagine trying to explain your GPS to Matthew. This simultaneously allows science fiction writers to cover a lot of ground without the story devolving into explanations—wild speculations—about how the future technology will work, but it also makes it more difficult for us to distinguish the science from the conjuring acts. Great science fiction tends to venture far out in its speculation, and the Magus may not have been entirely exiled from the literature. Two examples of sf authors playing with the sense of things not being quite what they seem are Philip K. Dick's *The Three Stigmata of Palmer Eldritch* (1965), a novel that bounces between an account of intrigues on Mars with its engineered fads and some truly strange and inexplicable happenings, and Ian Watson's *The Gardens of Delight* (1980), which introduces us to an unlikely partnership between an alchemist and an AI.

Indeed, the new Magus may not be a human character at all. Another Ian (McDonald) gives us some suspiciously mage-like AIs (here called *aeais)* in a near-future India, in his novel *River of Gods* (2007). Perhaps the reader will consider this too obvious; after all, AIs are *supposed* to possess awesome intelligence, aren't they? The tipping point in a story—for me at least—is when the machine demonstrates abilities and powers that seem inconceivable for humans to have programmed into it:

> How can I explain the perceptions of an aeai to a biological intelligence? [an aeai asks.] You're separate, contained. We are connected patterns and levels of subintelligences shared in common….
> I exist in many different physical spaces simultaneously. You have difficulty believing that. I have difficulty believing in your mortality. (p. 482)

Like a highly intelligent alien, a highly evolved AI is hard to distinguish from a Magus. Nor can we forget that Clarke himself gave us a non-human archetype of the Magus in the Monolith of *2001*. Hard to turn Jupiter into a star, however dim, by either magic or known science, but a Magus might pull it off!

At first glance, it would seem that in science fiction at least we have put away childish dreams. Yet the needs of the older parts of our brains aren't always rational; we still crave the encounter with things that can't be explained. I would suggest that just as we're not done yet with the ancient archetypes of the Hero or the Holy Fool, we should be on the lookout for the Magus, possibly on the bridge of a starship.

Sex, Skin, and Secret Messages

What is it that makes us entertain fantasies about mating outside our own species? Surely this can't be in our DNA; the mule, sterile offspring of a horse and donkey's mating, is an example of the evolutionary dead end that results. Yet since our earliest days we've apparently been fascinated by the non-human cultures we co-exist with, and the fantasy of strange creatures, able to shift from wild animal to human. Romeo and Juliet, our ancestors seem to have said, don't necessarily have to be of the same species. Long before we could write, we told stories around the campfire about strange creatures as lovers as well as monsters.

The hallmark of stories about the shape-shifting animal spouse is that both partners are mortal, they are each clearly one species not hybrids, and their interaction involves betrayal and suffering for one and sometimes both partners, sometimes physical, almost always emotional. I must leave out of the discussion immortal beings such as Zeus who adopt animal shapes in order to seduce human females, although those may be the wellspring of the myths I'm examining. Similarly, stories that portray creatures that are half-human and half-beast, such as satyrs, don't belong in this discussion. A subset of the animal-spouse stories in which the animal turns out to be under a spell (for instance, *Beauty and the Beast*, *The Princess and the Frog*, or *Swan Lake*) also lies outside this discussion. The werewolf, although obviously a shape-shifter, doesn't belong in this category either, since the turning point of werewolf stories has little to do with the betrayal of love, and the completely-human partner has no chance to trap the shape-shifter by stealing his skin. I would note that recent movies on the theme of love between werewolves/vampires and human females tend to blur the categories—and in so doing they manage to trivialize the deeper lessons of the shape-shifter myth.

Bruno Bettelheim wrote that fairy tales were the means by which human tribes handed down their accumulated wisdom to the next generation. They are not message-free; in fact, as with myths, the opposite is true; Cinderella's stepsisters pay dearly for their treachery, the wicked queen pays with her life for having tried to kill Snow White. In later centuries, we seem to have watered down the messages, especially in the post-Disney world, but the continuing popularity, even into our scientific age, of what might otherwise be considered mere nursery tales tells us that at least some of the original serious intention seems to be getting through.

Stories about animal spouses, shape-shifters, are not exempt from carrying messages, the most vivid of these being the warning against inter-species mating. The most iconic shape-shifter folk tales concern the selkie, the seal that lays its skin aside and becomes human for a period of time. Versions of this poignant tale of love between a human and a shape-shifting seal are to be found all over the North Atlantic where seals are familiar, particularly among the Celtic and Scandinavian peoples. In our time, movies such as *Ondine* (2009) and *The Secret of Roan Inish* (1994) are examples of retellings in a contemporary setting. In such tales, a human finds a selkie's skin on the beach and keeps it, thus trapping the unfortunate creature in its human shape. Most often, this is the result of the human falling in love with the selkie. Often compromise is reached with the selkie being allowed to return once a year to his or her home under the waves. Sometimes, the stories turn darker, and the human spouse hides or destroys the skin, thus trapping the selkie on land forever, which often results in the selkie pining away to death. Occasionally, this choice is made voluntarily when the selkie returns the human's love and makes the ultimate sacrifice. Bettelheim explains the power of these stories:

> It is characteristic of fairy tales to state an existential dilemma briefly and pointedly; this permits the child to come to grips with the problem in its most essential form.... Contrary to what takes place in many modern children's stories, evil is as omnipresent as virtue. (p. 8)

Selkie stories offer poignant examples of this dilemma: not just that we pay a price for falling under the spell of inappropriate love—a breaking of sexual taboo that would be sobering enough for the tribe's ultimate survival—but that nothing good comes from a bad action. The attempt to possess another in the name of love ends in betrayal. The finder of the selkie's skin condemns her (or, less commonly, him) to suffer and perhaps even to death by the very action of his love when he hides her skin in order to keep her, but the insightful psychological message of the ancient stories is even more interesting. We learn that not only the selkie suffers; *both* parties pay a steep emotional price as a consequence of breaking tribal sexual taboos.

The animal-spouse figure isn't limited to being a seal; folk literature is full of stories of deer, bears, badgers, and wolves shedding their skins to mate with humans.

Two recent examples of this theme in mainstream literature are John Straley's *The Woman Who Married a Bear* (1992) and Louise Erdrich's Native American story *The Antelope Wife* (1998). Not surprisingly, many modern fantasy writers have found fertile ground in such themes. Kij Johnson's *The Fox Woman* (2000), a sensitive re-imagining of a traditional Japanese version of the animal bride story, is a notable example:

> "He is a man," Grandfather said. "You are a fox. What did you expect? You smell of musk and carry vermin and you shit where you please."
>
> "You knew I had no hopes!… I cannot live like this," I said. "I will die."
>
> "There is one thing we can do," Mother said.
>
> "She means you can take human shape," my grandfather said wearily. (p. 133)

Johnson explores the theme that the pursuit of non-human sexual partners is a threat to human survival strategies, but it also reaffirms the ancient message that good intentions are no guarantee of good outcomes; both partners and their families suffer from the illicit liaison. Like all the best shape-shifter stories, it evokes wonder for the mystery of the other creatures sharing our world.

What of science fiction, which prides itself on a logical, non-magical view of things? We might expect that fantastic liaisons between human and beast would be missing from the canon, and indeed, the shape-shifting element seems to have fallen foul of the transfer of mass equations. Yet if we broaden the definition of "beast" to "non-human," including artificial constructs of various kinds and alien species, we see that as least as far back as Lester del Rey's "Helen O'Loy" (1938)—a robot—the genre was open to discussions about the possibilities of human/non-human partnership. Theodore Sturgeon, a much wiser writer than del Rey, contributed several memorable pieces involving inappropriate (i.e., non-species specific) attraction and the price that needs must be paid if emotion drives one's actions. I recommend that the reader start by taking a look at "Affair with a Green Monkey" (1953)—where not everything is as it seems to at least one of the characters—as an example.

More recent examples have remained true to the spirit of the ancient tragedy of impossible love between disparate species with its hard lessons. Tanith Lee's *The Silver Metal Lover* (1981) is strictly speaking not a shape-shifter story; although like Asimov's robot in "The Bicentennial Man" (1976), this metal creature yearns to be human, there is no chance of reverting to original form for either character. It's a modern use of the Romeo and Juliet plot, where the lovers come from species as different as human and robot. At least part of the power of Lee's story to move us is that we recognize the basic theme early on and know its inevitable tragic consequences, yet we hope anyway for matters to end well. We have been misled by Disney to believe that fairy tales always have happy endings. On the contrary, as Bettelheim points out, most of the original versions involve suffering and bloodshed, and in many tales, loss of all hope.

Recently I came across a science fiction story that embodies both the forbidden love aspect and the shape-shifter theme: "The Djinn's Wife" (2009) by Ian Mc-Donald. In a near-future India, a young entertainer falls in love with an "aeai's" avatar that materializes to compliment her on her dancing. An artificial intelligence isn't mortal, but neither is it a god. It's the ultimate shape-shifter, since an AI has no original shape but can manifest endless avatars:

Then the jets from the fountain ripple as if in the wind, but it is not the wind, not on this stifling afternoon, and the falling water flows into the shape of a man, walking out of the spray. A man of water that shimmers and flows and becomes a man of flesh. A. J. Rao. No, she thinks, never flesh. A djinn. A thing caught between heaven and hell. (p. 165)

The story of their impossible love and resulting marriage in violation of cultural taboo, plays out against a backdrop of a technologically advanced but ecologically ruined India. True to the spirit of the fairy tale and the myth, this version of inter-species attraction turns on traditional themes of possession, jealousy, and ultimately—betrayal.

I'm led to wonder whether our ancestors' developing consciousness, with its growing sense of the separation of self and other, played an early part in the construction of these narratives. Certainly, the loneliness of the human that comes from a sense of being shut-out from the natural world gave rise to the yearning to transcend the boundaries through sex, the primitive, emotional path of the heart, still in touch with that world. If so, then it became the task of the brain to argue against such a dangerous path. This is what science fiction does best, embodying the old tribal wisdom in new scientific clothes. There are no new stories, only old ones endlessly re-cast and re-told. The power we experience in stories is directly related to their grounding in much, much older myths and fairytales told by our ancestors at the dawn of history. Yearning for experience—including sexual—outside our normal human lives, we're attracted by the different, the taboo, to the extent that at times our passions overrule our common sense. Surely this will continue to be true even in a star-faring future. The more things change, apparently, the more they stay the same at their emotional core.

We've always known the secret message of the selkie: There's a steep price to pay for transcending the boundaries of the tribe. It probably won't stop us trying, anyway. After all, that's what makes us human.

Things that Go Bump
in the Dark

Strange creatures roam the streets of our neighborhoods once a year: monsters, ghosts, space creatures, and a few politicians. Halloween, we call it, and explain that although it has pagan origins, it also has a Christian overlay—or maybe we don't bother with that at all and just concentrate on the candy. Whatever we think of the holiday, it's a symptom of something that lies deep in human memory, our fear of, and attraction to, strangeness, otherness.

As a species, we seem to have always been fascinated by the monstrous. I imagine our cave-dwelling ancestors sitting around the fire, telling stories about the terrifying things that stalk by night. And surely, real predators like the Dire Wolf and the Sabertooth Tiger, eyes glowing in the dark forest, were scary enough to engender a host of cautionary tales about what happens to those who stray from the protection of the village fires. Perhaps racial memories of other, competing tribes so recently extinct, such as the Neanderthals gave rise to stories of the frightful creature that was almost but not quite human. The list of legendary fearsome creatures encountered around the world is diverse and long: sphinx, dragon, basilisk, lamia, gryphon, Sasquatch, Baba Yaga, yōkai—

every tribe has had its own favorite horror. The Greeks gave us myths about the Minotaur and the Cyclops, and Medusa with her head of snakes. In the centuries before science was able to explain away (for the most part) these horrifying creations, the myths in which they appeared exerted an endless pull on our imaginations. Part of the monsters' function was to keep people—especially children—in line. Rule-breaking, tradition-defying, laid one open to the predations of the unthinkable; worse, the tribe could be endangered. The power of these mythic beasts lay in the fact that they *could* be true, not that we always believed they were true.

The thing all these monsters have in common is that on some level they are images of ourselves, seen in a distorting mirror. Robert Louis Stevenson understood this when he gave us an early science fiction novel about Dr Jekyll and Mr Hyde (1886), two aspects of the same man, one admirable, one monstrous. The secret is that to be truly spine-chilling, there has to be an element of human reference in our monsters. It's not as scary to us if the monster figure does things completely outside our comprehension as it is if we can recognize some aspect of ourselves in its actions; otherwise, the monster is not likely to inhabit our nightmares for very long. The image of Hannibal Lector disturbs more sleep than that of Godzilla. But as science vanquished superstition, these strange children of the imagination lost their power to enthrall us, dwindling down to the scurrying forms on our streets at the end of October, accepting our token offerings of candy in exchange for a promise not to vandalize the property.

Most religions have given up threatening us with devils and demons, yet, like our ancestors, we still enjoy the frisson of terror, something that causes the rush of adrenaline that propels us into doing battle with our fears. Luckily for us, there is one species of monster that science hasn't forbidden us to believe in today; in fact science fosters the possibility of this creature being out there. Of course, I'm referring to the alien from space. Most of us have no more chance of meeting an alien than our ancestors had of meeting Grendel, but we are fascinated by tall tales just the same.

Perhaps this ambivalent reaction to that which is almost-but-not-quite-like-us gives us insight into one of the genre's first novels, Mary Shelley's *Frankenstein*. While the scientist in the story regards his creation as a monster, and the other characters react with fear and outrage, the reader's sympathy is more likely to be divided. We recognize aspects of our own humanity in the monster who doesn't even have a name:

> I am malicious because I am miserable. Am I not shunned and hated by all mankind? You, my creator, would tear me to pieces, and triumph; remember that, and tell me why I should pity man more than he pities me? Shall I respect man when he contemns me? Let him live with me in the interchange of kindness; and, instead of injury, I would bestow every benefit upon him with tears of gratitude. (p. 128)

The monster yearns to be human, to be accepted, to learn and do good to others, but that only succeeds in making him more horrifying; it's not long before the villagers turn on him.

I believe it's this almost-but-not-quite aspect that gives life to the most terrifying monsters. This uncomfortable shock of recognizing ourselves and our actions in something totally unlike us is what drove the panic and hysteria that accompanied the radio broadcast of Orson Welles' version of H. G. Wells' *The War of the Worlds*

(1898). Wells' aliens might not physically resemble us, but we could certainly believe that visitors from another planet had only conquest on their minds. We would've done the same thing if the tables had been turned—indeed *had* done in the recent conquests of empire.

Obviously, the monster's proper home in the genre is the related field of horror where the author can pull out all the stops to scare the breath out of us. There is little or no need in horror stories for a logical explanation of how the monster came to be; terror is uncontaminated by logic. But in science fiction the author is expected to explain the frightful in terms of the mundane, scientific world we inhabit or have cause to presume we may inhabit in the future.

To my mind, one of the most satisfying monsters in recent science fiction film is the alien that Sigourney Weaver's character, Ripley, faces in *Alien* (1979). One thing movies can do well is build believable, frightening creatures, and this alien is visually one of the most successful. But I think that's not why it comes across to us as genuinely terrifying. When we analyze the basis for its shocking actions, we can identify several elements that we recognize from our own experience, although it's nothing like us physically. This monster is female; she nurtures her young—albeit by inserting them into nutritional hosts, just as some Earth insects use unwilling "foster mothers" from other species. She protects her young by killing those who might menace them; we can understand that protective instinct. She seeks revenge when her young are killed, a very human-like reaction. That's what stimulates the most ancient part of our brains, raising our atavistic hackles. It's like looking into a distorting mirror of extreme aspects of ourselves. The sight of a Godzilla-clone destroying yet another city may be thrilling, but it doesn't evoke the same recognition or the same terror.

The most disturbing science fiction about aliens relies on this psychological mechanism to cause horror in the reader. Octavia Butler's "Bloodchild" (1984) poses a terrifying choice for its main character: accept his stomach-turning symbiotic destiny with the alien and lose his freedom (and perhaps his life), or deny it and escape but never thrive nor find peace:

> I had been told all my life that this was a good and necessary thing Tlic and Terran did together—a kind of birth. I had believed it until now. I knew birth was painful and bloody, no matter what. But this was something else, something worse. (p. 506)

It's important for us to understand that the aliens in this story that cause the dilemma are not evil, and the bonds between them and the humans are about nurturing and love, very human aspirations. The real horror is that on some level we not only understand but come to sympathize with the monstrous aliens who face extinction without human cooperation.

As Gregory Benford remarks, "The problem with aliens is that they're alien." Terry Carr's previously mentioned story, "The Dance of the Changer and the Three," gives us an apparently friendly alien that unpredictably destroys an entire human colony for ultimately inscrutable reasons. This is a fascinating, well-told story, but it lacks the chilling power of Butler's tale, not because its aliens are energy-beings rather than carbon-based life-forms, but because their psychology isn't remotely similar to ours. We find nothing in them to identify with; they remain intellectually interesting to us, not viscerally terrifying. Similarly, I find the Berserkers, marauding machine intelligences that inhabit Fred Saberhagen's series of stories about alien invasion, frightening to contemplate—how could mere humans hope to survive against them?—but not blood-curdlingly terrifying because there are so few points of reference. Their predations are scary to think about, but not bone-chilling experiences of terror.

When the monsters, mythic or alien, share many physical characteristics with us but not all, then we enter what's known as the spooky territory of the "uncanny valley." The term was invented by Masahiro Mori, a professor of robotics, to map the point at which puppets and robots, constructed with increasingly realistic human faces, fall into an area where they cause revulsion instead of empathy from viewers. Many moviegoers objected to the animated children's film *The Polar Express* (2004) because the characters, especially the train's conductor, were drawn just a little bit *off* the human norm, but not enough to make them recognizably, and non-threateningly, cartoons. The resulting oddness set a number of viewers' teeth on edge. I think the reaction many children and some adults have to circus clowns may be based on this same "uncanny valley" sensation.

The wonderful story by C. L. Moore described earlier understands this eerie boundary. It's not about a monster at all, but about a beautiful dancer, hopelessly disfigured in a fire, and reconstructed with all her memories and abilities in a delicate, scintillating robot body. Deirdre, in "No Woman Born," is described through the eyes of a former admirer who finds himself in the uncanny valley, attracted and repelled in equal measure by what remains of the Deirdre he knew and what she has become. The story evokes both the myth of the phoenix rising from the fire that consumes it, and that of the Greek sculptor whose ivory statue is brought to life by a sympathetic goddess; Pygmalion appears here as the scientist Maltzer, creating the work of beauty Deirdre becomes. It derives much of its power through its poetic, metaphor-laden prose just as Bradbury's work does. This resurrected Deirdre may not be a classic monster, but she isn't someone you'd feel comfortable being around for long:

> "I can't go and leave you—not understanding," [Maltzer said]. "It would be even worse than the thought of your failure, to think of you bewildered and confused when the mob turns on you…. You're not wholly human, my dear."
> (p. 181)

Our modern monsters, whether from outer space or the scientific laboratory down the road, may not resemble the creatures that haunted the Greeks' nightmares, but the mechanism by which these constructs of the imagination attract and repel us remains the same. The trick for the writer or film-maker is to give us an alien that is menacing enough to be scary while still remaining understandable to us on an emotional, empathic level. No robotic storm-trooper or Terminator can cause the chill that runs down our spines like the image of our own humanity seen in the distorting mirror of the alien. The penalty for not taking the threat of the monster seriously may be as dire to us in the modern world as it was to our cave-dwelling ancestors.

Islands of the Imagination

The allure of islands finds its way into both our earliest myths and stories and our most-recent science fiction: Odysseus on the island of Circe the sorceress; Blackbeard in the Caribbean; Robinson Crusoe's island, Treasure Island. The names chime in the imagination like poetry: Hebrides and Seychelles; Easter Island and Christmas Island; the poignant beauty of the line "where the remote Bahamas ride," of the seventeenth century poet Andrew Marvell, recalls the emotional pull of the island in our imaginations. No wonder Shakespeare set *The Tempest* (1611), his most magical play, on an island. Thomas More's *Utopia* (1516) was set on an island of that name, and a recent novel by Christopher Priest, *The Islanders* (2011), recounts the interwoven, mysterious and dreamlike histories of a whole archipelago of islands (more on this novel later).

An island is a world entire in itself, full of fabulous possibilities for a better life, or for dark deeds best performed away from scrutiny; sometimes, the island becomes a laboratory, isolated and protected from the intrusions of the everyday world. Not surprising then that many science fiction writers should be inspired to use island settings for their imaginations to populate. H. G. Wells described stomach-churning secret experiments turning animals into men taking place on *The Island of*

Doctor Moreau (1896), and in doing so, subverted the mythic version of men turned into beasts that Odysseus encountered on Circe's island. Islands are important in works such as C. S. Lewis's *Perelandra* (1943), and in more modern literature, Sir Arthur C. Clarke's tales of space stations and orbiting colonies, described as islands in the sky, *The Fountains of Paradise* (1979). China Miéville describes lashed-together boats that form a floating island in *The Scar* (2002). All of these works allow the author a protected space to work out theories and speculations, away from the constraints of normal life, even as it is mirrored in fiction. Hollywood has used the isolated island as setting for many science fictional or horror tales, one of the most recent being *Shutter Island* (2010).

The metaphor of the island in science fiction can be prison or safe haven, the isolation it affords either good or bad. Or as J. G. Ballard once remarked, "The Island is a state of mind." Setting a story on an island allows the writer to break free of the strictures of existing societies with their heavy load of historical influence and their pressure toward mimetic fiction rather than imaginative. The writer becomes free to perform the kind of pure *gedankenexperimenten* that Einstein used effectively. Stanislaw Lem's *Solaris* (1961) gives us a planet-wide intelligence that creates islands, a good example of the island as thought experiment: How would we deal with this truly, perhaps malignantly, alien being without losing our grip on reality? Hilbert Schenck gives us another in *A Rose for Armageddon* (1982) where we are invited to speculate about space-time and transcendence in a way not possible in a non-island setting where the mundane world holds sway.

Gathering my lingster stories together for the collection *The Guild of Xenolinguists* (2007), I was bemused to find how islands had crept into more than one of them. (Perhaps this fascination isn't so surprising since I was born on one.) I couldn't have written "No Brighter Glory" (1999) if it hadn't been set on an island; the emotional attraction of the island for the protagonist, who was born in the Hebrides, and the isolation it afforded the antagonist to pursue an unethical experiment gave rise to the plot. And I see now that a lot of mythic influences came together in another island story, "Stranger Than Imagination Can" (2007). From the moment I realized that my crew were heading to a world orbiting a star with the impressive-sounding (but fictitious) Messier catalog number NGC312150, called "Prospero" after the astronomer who found it, I knew I was dealing with Shakespeare. True to its Elizabethan inspiration, *The Tempest,* the beautiful but apparently empty archipelago on my planet was filled with mysterious music and mischievous spirits, with a perhaps deadly purpose at its heart. An island isn't always a benign paradise, even if it seems so at first, and Shakespeare's Prospero was not above making mortals suffer. Isolated from the vast accumulation of human philosophy and technology, and with no alien culture to examine for answers, I freed my characters to learn that the universe may be stranger (and more dangerous) than we can imagine, a philosophy that many myths teach us.

There is something dreamlike about stories set on islands, and Priest's novel about the Dream Archipelago, which I referred to earlier, is a notable example. In this case, Priest has invented a whole series of islands, all of them with detailed geographies and histories, flora and fauna, currency and customs, all of them linked to each other and at the same time contradictory—and mysterious:

> The problems of mapping the Dream Archipelago are well understood. High altitude aerial

> cartography is more or less impossible because of the distortion caused by the temporal gradients. These gradients…exist in every part of the world except at the magnetic poles. Even within a few degrees of these poles, which of course are in frozen land areas, the variations in what can be observed or photographed make reliable charting inconsistent and therefore unfeasible. (p. 8)

The combination of guidebook-like descriptions of the geography and the culture of the separate islands in the archipelago with the fantasy element of imprecision caused by "temporal distortion" allows Priest to endow his story with far more layers of meaning than he could have achieved with a more mundane setting.

All stories set on islands take advantage of the isolation that stems from separation from the neighboring continent to allow non-linear development to happen; each island is an invitation for social experimentation. (Remember that Ursula K. Le Guin's fantasy quartet that included the novel referred to earlier, *A Wizard of Earthsea,* is also set on an archipelago.) Priest magnifies this effect by the number of islands in his fictitious archipelago, while at the same time ensuring that they are linked by their stories in ways that are sometimes explicit (a clue to an apparent murder on one island may be found in a story about another) and sometimes tantalizingly amorphous. Since the novel is set up in the manner of a gazetteer containing information that might be of use to tourists, we are encouraged to indulge the fantasy of setting sail for these islands that may or may not exist at the edge of their world.

Science fiction writers and readers like to find answers and solve problems; such fiction is didactic in purpose to the extent that science fiction is always concerned with the idea of what may-yet-be, far more so than is mainstream, mimetic fiction. An island setting offers a useful laboratory. Perhaps it's no coincidence that we've become more concerned with the health of our planet since the astronauts looked back from the Moon and saw this island Earth floating alone in the dark sea of space. Yet analysis of the political and psychological symbolism of islands aside, there remains their purely visceral and perhaps atavistic tug at our emotions. I think of those early humans, our ancestors, on their long migration out of Africa at the dawn of history, coming to the edge of the world as they understood it and facing the daunting power of the sea. They must have experienced exhaustion, hunger, and thirst on their trek through jungles and across deserts; they would have been hunted by fierce animals and maybe by other species in the humanoid family. And on the horizon, perhaps there rose the silhouette of an island promising safety, shelter, a new beginning, if only they could use that newly-developing brain to figure out a way to get there.

It might as well have been our descendants, gazing at a world a whole galaxy away.

Old Man River

The Los Angeles and the San Gabriel Rivers that form the western and eastern boundaries of Long Beach, where I live, have been tamed. Concrete-channeled, laden with trash after a rainstorm from careless upstream cities, they empty into the Pacific like sad puppies let out to relieve themselves, a far cry from the wild beauty of their bigger brethren around the world. Gazing at these subdued California waterways, I find it depressing to remember that lost rivers such as these once played important roles in human history, not the least being the lifeblood of the community dependent on its life-giving floods that replenished the parched fields of desert kingdoms. Rivers formed the first interstate highways. The river of my youth, the Thames, provided a route for kings and queens traveling between the royal residences at Hampton Court, Westminster, and Greenwich.

Beyond their practical aspects, in human imagination rivers have always been powerful symbols. Our blood stream is a river in itself, so it's no wonder the river's passage from spring in the mountains to final emptying into the ocean came to be a metaphor for life from birth to death. Psychoanalytic dream analysis recognizes this numinous quality of rivers; they are often considered to reveal unconscious secrets of the dreamer's life. Rivers appear in the myths and legends of almost every tribe on the planet, the Tigris and the Euphrates that bounded Eden, the Jordan where Christ was baptized, the Tiber on whose banks the Twins founded Rome, the life-giving Nile, the jungle-hearted Amazon, the sacred Ganges. Not surprisingly, we find writers as diverse as Thoreau, T. S. Eliot, and Mark Twain using rivers as metaphors for the passage of a life in their work. This metaphoric use of a river setting turns up in children's literature, too. One notable example occurs in Kenneth Grahame's novel *The Wind in the Willows* (1908), where the cast of Rat, Badger, Mole and Toad spend hours puttering about on the river, thereby imparting a lot of life's wisdom to the readers.

A brief glance at a catalog of science fiction titles seems to indicate an equal fascination in our genre. Gregory Benford's *Great Sky River* (1987)—the road of souls for many Native American tribes—invokes the Milky Way Galaxy streaming overhead. In Philip Jose Farmer's series of novels collectively called Riverworld (1971-83), the resurrected likes of Mark Twain, Sir Richard Burton, and Jack London (explorers all) set out to learn the purpose and the contours of this alien-constructed universe in the form of a gigantic, all-encompassing river, with increasing chaos as the consequence.

Considered as metaphor, in European usage the source of the river symbolizes birth, and the mouth symbolizes our re-absorption back into the All, the direction of the flow being the natural path of human life. So what are we to make of stories about going upriver, against the current? It might be logical to expect them to carry themes of a return to childhood innocence, but instead they seem to reflect just the opposite, the warning Thomas Wolfe gave us, "You can't go home again." Return to the womb is neither possible nor to be aspired to, upriver journeys tell us, especially when we realize nations follow the same path from a state of primitive existence to a later, more socialized one that human life follows. "Upriver" comes to symbolize devolution not evolution of the human spirit.

Joseph Conrad's novel *Heart of Darkness* (1899), where a journey up the Congo, from the teeming civilization of the European-colonized African coast to an earlier state of humanity in the jungle, reveals the depravity of the colonizers and the breakdown of ivory-trader Kurtz's psyche. "Going native" here means much more than wearing Earth-friendly cotton and necklaces of seed pods, or avoiding fast food and pesticides. This novel has become the inspiration for others that have attempted to explore the same theme: the darkness that lies at the heart of "civilized" humanity. All our pious sophistication and our elaborate manners and customs, such novels tell us, are only a thin skin over a raging horror of out-of-control appetites and evil intent. Conrad's narrator, Marlowe, whose job it is to bring back Kurtz, sees little innocence in the well-spring of our dark hearts.

Francis Ford Coppola's 1979 movie, *Apocalypse Now*, set against the backdrop of the Vietnam War, remains true to this motif; Captain Willard travels upriver deep into the jungle to encounter his own "Kurtz," a once-admirable man who has "gone native" in all the worst senses of the phrase. But it isn't just Kurtz who has endangered his soul; society too stands to lose as the result of the devolution of morals and ethics that result from this jungle war. The theme of a person losing the tenuous hold civilization has on humans, and becoming more influenced by amoral (to say the least) circumstances the further upriver one travels, is explored in another movie: *The Mosquito Coast*, based on Paul Theroux's novel of the same name (1986). Allie Fox is a genius, a likable man when we first meet him, who conceives the plan to travel upriver deep into the jungle to build an ice house to supply the natives with a valuable product. But "upriver" seduces decent, capable men; they go from being helpers to exploiters, and eventually, like Allie Fox, they go mad. *Apocalypse Now* goes one step further, adding the somber message that such men must be killed for the common good.

It's not exaggeration to say that all three of these tales can be read as metaphors for the dangers advanced societies experience in contact with what they patronizingly consider "primitive." All three versions of the going upriver theme warn us that we have no business feeling superior to those we perceive as less far along on the path than we are, or attempting to patronize them "for their own good," or assuming we will regain some of our lost innocence by this venture. Doing so, we are warned, we court disaster and death for ourselves and ultimately for our "advanced, civilized" societies.

Science fiction extends the river journey into space. The basic assumption in sf tends to be that if we arrive on the aliens' planet first, then we are the superior race; if the aliens land on Earth first, then we are in danger of being treated in much the same way we've behaved in our history of exploration and colonization. Robert Silverberg's novel *Downward to the Earth* (1970), which references Conrad's novel (including the name Kurtz) explores much the same mythic territory. In a story that evokes humanity's often disastrous colonial past, going upriver on an Eden-like alien planet doesn't result in greater innocence or humanity of spirit for the protagonist; instead, the opposite is true. The main character, Gunderson, violates the belief and customs of the planet's inhabitants for his own gain because he deems them of lesser value, and in doing so risks his own spiritual integrity. Myths are always didactic, even in science fictional versions, so we shouldn't be surprised to find lessons along with story. Silverberg's novel offers a new perspective on the "going upriver" theme, warning us not to export our questionable values around the galaxy.

Sometimes, the journey upriver is a minor part of a larger myth being used in a story. This is the case when the human explorers travel the river road deeper into alien territory in Mary Doria Russell's *The Sparrow*, examined previously, Russell uses the river journey to illustrate the gradual breakdown of the influence of human civilization on the characters, preparing us for the horrors of the Jesuit priest's later experience. And sometimes the river flows through the novel, underlining all the history, the culture, the hopes, dreams, fears of the story itself, as the Ganges in all its polluted glory does in Ian McDonald's *River of Gods*:

> Shiv's never seen the river so low…he is uncomfortable, like blood gushing from a wound in the arm of an old friend that you cannot heal…. Five seasons ago, he had been a river kid, squatting by the smudge-fire, poking along the sand, sifting the silt for rags and pickings. He'll end up there too, sometime. Shiv will end up there. It's a thing he's always known. Everyone ends up there. The river bears all away. Mud and skulls. (p. 12)

Other writers use the river as a metaphor for the vision of life or the future that the novel sets out to unfold. Nicola Griffith's *Slow River* (1995) opens with a compelling view of a river flowing through a city that I could easily have used to introduce this discussion:

> Rivers were the source of civilization, the scenes of all beginnings and endings in ancient times. Babies were carried to the banks to be washed,

> bodies were laid on biers and floated away. Births and deaths were usually communal affairs, but I was here alone. (p. 3)

But the archetypal river of this pastoral opening scene gives way to another, more ominous stream, that of sewage and pollutants raging through a treatment plant, itself a metaphor for the degraded, dangerous state of life in this now and future world:

> The roar became a bellow, a deep chasm of noise, old and ugly, big enough to grind its way through the crust of the world. I clapped my hands over my ears, but the noise was a living thing, battering at my ribs, vibrating my skull. We stood at the edge of the pit where water rushed past, twisting and boiling. It was like standing on the edge of creation. (p. 45)

It's instructive to compare these two passages about two very different rivers. Griffith's first description is almost mythic in its images of birth and death, community and civilization; contrast this with the second "river" and note the menacing choice of words and metaphors Griffith uses, "roar," "bellow," "grind," "battering," and "boiling," and the simile "like standing on the edge of creation." If the first river Griffith describes is the River Jordan, then the second is the River Styx.

The river journey transcends everybody's history and expands into our future, a Jungian theme that speaks not of our past but of our soul. It shouldn't surprise us to find this same use of the river theme in science fiction, a literature that ostensibly deals with our potential future but also with the fate of our very humanity.

Ghost Riders in the Sky

I was a young teenager in London, listening to American 78 rpm records when Tennessee Ernie Ford's version of this haunting ballad became popular. The story of cowboys cursed to chase their thundering herds of cattle across the sky forever was fascinating and somehow chilling; I played the record over and over until my mother complained. The nightmare image seemed almost familiar, though it was years before I encountered its ghostly ancestor, The Wild Hunt. Humans probably began to believe in ghosts and hauntings soon after they evolved enough of a forebrain to mourn the past and plan for the future. Certainly we know that Ancient Greeks, Romans, Egyptians, and Chinese took reports of ghosts seriously, believing them to be harbingers of unpleasant fates waiting to torment them. In the Christian Era, an important variation occurred with the story of the man who mocked Christ's journey to Gethsemane and was therefore condemned to never die but wander the Earth as punishment.(I noted the appearance of this figure earlier, as he wanders through the pages of *A Canticle for Leibowitz*.) The Wandering Jew was later joined by the Flying Dutchman, another cursed member of the Undying. This combination of ghostly hunters, the Undying and Death itself, is a potent brew capable of provoking our nightmares.

The phantasmal hunt version of this theme comes down to us in the west by way of Old Norse mythology where the god Wodan or Odin thundered across the sky on his eight-legged steed, Sleipnir, hunting and berserking. It was reinforced by the tale of the Valkyries and gained power in the story of Ragnarok, or The Twilight of the Gods, when Loki and the enemies of the gods came galloping on their magical steeds over the rainbow bridge to bring down Odin's home. Certainly there are also elements of racial memory operating here; anywhere there has been violent conquest, the echoes of marauding parties and bloodthirsty armies will be found in the folk lore that emerges. Versions of this tale are found all across Europe, where such violence was a fact of life for many generations; medieval villagers believed they could hear the pounding hooves in the darkest part of the year and thought it safer to hide indoors. The echoes of this racial memory are the cause of the chills we experience in the movie *Apocalypse Now,* when Coppola, who deliberately made reference to the mythic theme of "going upriver," has the attacking Hueys rising like a pack of dark hunters over the brow of a hill to the accompaniment of Wagner's "The Ride of the Valkyries."

As centuries passed and memories of Viking raids and Viking lore faded, the names changed. "Cain's Hounds," they were called in parts of Europe, and "Gabriel's Hounds" in parts of England, but the idea that the ghostly hunter and his hounds were cursed clung to the story. The chief hunter acquired the name "Herne" in Southern English village tales, possibly by way of the Celtic god Cernunnos, but perhaps from the Greek Orion, another mythic hunter in the sky. Herne was often depicted sporting a pair of horns, and we might speculate on the similarity of this figure to the "horned shaman" depicted on Paleolithic caves in Southern France.

Over time, the dread gradually faded out of the story until we arrive at Shakespeare's depiction of the shaming of old, lecherous Falstaff, made to wear "Herne's horns" in *The Merry Wives of Windsor*. And we've probably all played the childhood games of hunter and prey, known to us more benignly as "Catch" and "Hide and Seek," where the skills needed by our long-dead ancestors are still practiced. But where the legend persisted in its original menacing form, it was regarded as the worst of luck to witness the Wild Hunt thundering across the sky in search of prey; at the very least, racial memory said, it was a harbinger of the imminent approach of war or other disaster.

Not surprisingly, this theme has turned up in a lot of modern high fantasy, where it often blends with other fairy tale themes of the treachery of faerie and the unhappy fate of humans unlucky enough to draw the attention of the supernatural. The poet John Masefield described the Wild Hunt, with Death its leader, in "The Hounds of Hell" (1917):

> And trotting scatheless through the gorse
> And bristling in the fell,
> Lord, it is death upon the horse,
> And they're the hounds of hell!

In J. R. Tolkien's *The Lord of the Rings* (1954), the Dead Men of Dunharrow are a ghostly force that rides out on spectral horses in answer to Aragorn's call, terrifying all who encounter them, and finally winning their own release as a result. The Wild Hunt (or at least, a demon hunter of souls) appears in Philip Pullman's *Count Karlstein* (1982) and Peter Beagle's Young Adult ghost story *Tamsin* (1999) involves an American teenager and an English ghost, who have to deal with the spectral hunters active again in modern Dorset. Charles de Lint has even gone so far as to turn the huntsmen into motor-cycle riders and their horses into Harley-Davidsons in the fantasy novel *Jack the Giant-Killer* (1987), where the conflict between good and evil in the realms of faerie plays out against a backdrop of modern Canada.

Why should this myth hold any attraction for modern minds for whom the hunt is only something our ances-tors did because meat didn't come from the supermarket in their day, and for whom marauding armies happen to somebody else? What is it about this image that still manages to chill us? One clue is that the true prey of the Great Hunt is always sentient, in other words us, or our proxies. Traces of myth and archetype survive in pres-ent day literature because they carry an emotional weight that can underscore the theme of the work that invokes them. The story that manages to evoke a sense of the numinous increases its effectiveness for the reader who may not always be aware of why he or she is so affect-ed by the work. So it's not surprising that we find ver-sions—or at the very least, a trace—of another powerful theme, the uncanny hunters, underlying works that are more science fiction than fantasy, though transformed as befits a technological society poised to travel to the stars. Three notable examples are worth discussing.

The protagonist in Sheri Tepper's *Grass* (1989), Mar-jorie Westriding, an Olympic equestrian, comes to the planet Grass seeking to unlock the secret of the plan-et's immunity to a devastating plague that has raged on Earth. Tepper builds a genteel society here that evokes Earth's past, including the custom of riding horses to the fox hunt, accompanied by fox hounds. The aristocratic humans, known as "bons," who are already here have developed a form of hunting that involves a vicious spe-cies named "Hippae" (which is probably rooted in the Greek word for horse, but also making use of the fiercer connotations of the hippopotamus). The prey species, known as "foxen," we come to learn later are sentient, a fact the bons are aware of. The moral question this evokes is debated by the newcomers and the religious members of the Friary of the Green Brothers, another detail that reinforces the richness of references to an aristocratic past on Earth. This sport manages also to evoke the uneasy shiver of the spectral Wild Hunt in scenes where bons on horseback and the monstrous Hippae relentlessly pursue their sentient prey across the grassy prairies that give the novel its name. The scene, as Tepper draws it, deliberately reminds us of paintings of the peaceful English landscape, where the gentry, male and female, exquisitely outfitted and astride beautiful horses, take part in the bloody ritual of killing the small fox. And behind that again lie ancestral memories of villagers being overrun by waves of marauding enemies, in this case the Hippae who are just as likely to turn on the human hunters:

> The hounds were the size of Terran horses, muscled like lions, with broad, triangular heads and lips curled back to display jagged ridges of bone or tooth. Herbivores, Rigo thought at first. And yet there were fangs at the front of those jaws. Omnivores? (p. 104)

A work already discussed, Joan Vinge's *The Snow Queen,* gives us the character of the queen's champion/consort, Starbuck, whose real name is Herne, a hunter who leads a pack of nightmare-like hounds on a hunt to harvest a life-extending fluid from a race of gentle sea creatures; unbeknownst to queen and champion, these creatures are highly intelligent, and the hunt is exterminating them. We are led to suppose that even understanding this might not be enough for the queen to call off the hunt. Thus our sense of horror is doubly called into play. In both these novels, the author relies on our almost instinctive reaction to the symbol of the Hounds of Hell and their prey.

Gregory Benford's *Against Infinity* (1983)—a novel that the author has said is strongly influenced by William Faulkner's *The Bear*—is also about the hunt that is more than just a hunt. Like the two novels just discussed, this is a work of undeniable "hard" science fiction that combines the hunt theme with another, the "coming-of-age" story. Here, on an icy Ganymede in the process of being colonized, the mythic Hunt is turned on its head and reduced to one alien creature that in its ability to bring death and havoc to humans might as well be Death himself. Thirteen-year-old Manuel Lopez who sets out to succeed where adults have failed is the latest fictional representative of a long line of young, innocent Heroes whose mythic quest is to conquer the Death-bringing monster and release the community from its predations. Though the story is compelling on its own terms, the presence of the numinous looms over the narrative; an older part of our brain responds without our quite knowing why. (I think it's more than coincidence that some reviewers complained that after the alien is killed and the hunt theme is relinquished, the last part of the book loses its power.)

Perhaps even Frank Herbert's *Dune*, where humans pursue the giant sandworms of Arrakis, can be considered a version of the Great Hunt story; certainly the legendary trope is an integral part of the story, if not the whole of it. We in the urban West no longer live in a world of hunters and prey, but the nightmare presence of things over which we have no control can still haunt us, whether we think of them as supernatural or alien. As Jung pointed out, we may refuse to acknowledge the wisdom of myths, but we are nevertheless subject to the power they wield in our subconscious, and sometimes we sense the presence of the numinous even when we deny it exists.

The Feral Child

Archetypes, as Jung said, are part of the tribe's collective unconscious; they are manifestations of the human psyche, but not subject to or arising from the individual day-to-day experience of our early ancestors. Not all archetypes are found in myths, though many of them are. Myths are timeless and transcendent, and unlike legends, which are one-time stories of non-recurring events, these stories concern that which is immortal and ever-recurring. They may be entertaining—and to our twenty-first-century minds, quaintly simplistic as explanations of natural phenomena—but first and foremost, they are didactic in that they embody the collective wisdom of the tribe, a kind of user's manual for right living. In this they resemble fairy tales, their more homely and less exalted kin, which contain their own quota of life lessons and easily recognizable archetypes.

So far, I've focused on the idea that far from having outlived their usefulness, these archetypes re-appear in stories about the future—the Magus, the Holy Fool, the Mother Goddess, the Hero, and so on—and speculated about the source of their peculiar appeal to us over the millennia. These archetypes exert power in the unconscious such that we react to the figure and its story without always fully understanding why. Another such long-lived archetypal character is the Feral Child.

The feral child shows up very early in literature, for instance Enkidu who emerges from the forest to befriend Gilgamish in a Babylonian/Assyrian epic composed sometime between the latter half of the third and the earlier half of the second millennium BCE. The emotional origin of the theme of the lost child appears to be the result of a parental nightmare: the child lost in the dangerous primeval forest that surrounded vulnerable human settlements. Every child is precious to a small, threatened group, for in the next generation lies the survival of the species; a large percentage of the babies born to ancient tribes eventually succumbed to illnesses and accidents or were taken by predators. Not only the parents would be affected by such a loss. If it takes a village to raise a child, then a whole village will mourn the loss of its potential.

There's more to these stories than just playing on parental fears of loss. The feral child story delivers major psychological compensation because its central character not only doesn't perish, but is also nurtured by animals and often returns to the tribe with his innocence intact and with a wealth of animal lore and wisdom the tribe might potentially use. We get strong forms of this tradition in the Roman story of Romulus and Remus, Rudyard Kipling's Mowgli, Edgar Rice Burroughs' Tarzan, all of them children lost or abandoned and raised by forest creatures, with wolves and apes being the favored candidates. Versions of this theme appear in many of the world's myths and legends, for one example, the Hawai'ian story of the cast-out baby Princess Laieeikawai raised in a cavern that can only be reached by diving deep into a pond. As a weaker form, we can consider James Barrie's Peter Pan an aspect of the Feral Child; although he didn't grow up in a forest, he's certainly a lost boy whose innocent wisdom has turned to mischief. (An interesting play on this theme occurs in a recent movie, director Wes Anderson's *Moonlight Kingdom* [2012], where the young run-aways display an innocent wisdom unknown to the adults in the story, eventually returning—along with a now supportive Boy Scout troop—to civilization in the form of family life.)

There's an overlap here with the traditional mythology of the Hero, who often has dubious or unknown parentage and grows up outside the boundaries of his society, returning to become a savior of his people; King Arthur and Luke Skywalker are obvious examples, neither of whom was literally lost. Similarly, not all feral children become Hero figures; however, the Roman twins raised by a wolf show that it is possible to be both.

The return of the lost child and the resultant acquisition of animal lore is a story grieving parents want to believe in, for obvious reasons. But underlying this is a deep belief that humans possess from birth an innate moral sense that all too often is conditioned and corrupted by society or religion. I suspect this reflects the uneasiness felt by our ancestors as the simpler life in the forest or on the veldt gave way to life in the village and then the city, far more complex and confusing if not actually toxic for humans. Our own more cynical age has rejected this view of the natural state of moral purity corrupted by civilization, giving us works like William Golding's *Lord of the Flies* (1954) in which well-behaved young schoolboys revert to savagery as a result of becoming castaways on a deserted island.

The rather more modern question of the relative importance of nature or nurture in a person's subsequent behavior is a continuation of this ancient argument. Perhaps we hear echoes of the loss of Paradise here (itself an archetype), in the belief in primal innocence and goodness, and the resultant yearning to be reunited with the rest of the natural world. The returning feral child is seen as free of the moral corruption that is inevitable growing up in society, one who will bring back a lost purity to the tribe. This can prove a heavy burden on the child, and some fictional feral children (Mowgli, Peter Pan) find the task of restoring purity to the tribe too burdensome, the fellowship of humans inferior to that of animals, and they return to the jungle.

There is common ground between this archetype and another one that emerged later in western literature. The Noble Savage had its roots in Alexander Pope's "Essay on Man" (1734) and became increasingly popular in the eighteenth century. This archetype was developed in Jean-Jacques Rousseau's political philosophy of the same period. The more civilization expanded, or perhaps more correctly, industrialization and the resulting national need to spread into previously undeveloped territory, the more people yearned for the legendary innocence of the past displayed in the perceived behavior of the world's indigenous populations just then being "discovered." The irony here is that at the same moment the "primitive" is being celebrated, it is also being obliterated, a theme we find frequently in science fiction. In Ursula Le Guin's novella "The Word for World is Forest" (1976), we sympathize with the beleaguered native race on the planet, in deep communion and cooperation with their environment, who are enslaved and in danger of being wiped out by the greed of invading humans. James Cameron's film *Avatar* follows the same theme. The message is clear in both cases: If only we can learn from the lost secrets of the more innocent and natural past, we might be saved from the destruction we bring on them and ourselves.

Dozens of tales of real-life feral children found all over the world still intrigue us, among them Wild Peter,

Memmie le Blanc, Kasper Hauser, and Victor the Wild Child of Avalon, the subject of a film by Francois Truffaut, *L'Enfant Sauvage* (1970). Fostering animals are reputed to include wolves, apes, bears, dogs, monkeys, and birds. For centuries in Europe, a hairy "Wild Man" was a staple of traveling circuses and freak-shows, demonstrating the continuing power of this figure to enthrall our imaginations. Unlike their legendary counterparts, however, such real-life lost or abandoned children never learn to communicate fluently if they have had no human contacts to model speech during their early years, and their subsequent lives are for the most part unhappy and uninstructive.

The primeval forest vanished from most areas of our planet centuries ago, so what accounts for the continuing power of this archetype? If the surrounding forest and jungle are the backdrop for the myths and legends of our early ancestors, then the frontier—equally as dangerous—becomes the setting for legends told by tribes on the move. Children can get lost on the trek just as easily as they can from the village in the middle of the forest. And a society that considers space the "final frontier" will resonate to the archetype of the feral child just as those early Babylonians and Romans did.

In addition to those accidentally lost, science fiction adds those who are deliberately cast out, subjects of experiments, or the survivors of some form of apocalypse who embody a precious spirit the current world has lost and needs to regain. Aldous Huxley uses the first iteration of the ancient theme in *Brave New World* (1932); here, the wild child, John, was born and grew up outside of the civilization of bio-engineered humans and encounters it for the first time with innocent and, to our way of thinking, wise eyes. Huxley's view of the degeneracy of this civilization is apparent in that, far from valuing the gifts the Wild Child brings back, it destroys him.

The most famous example of this theme in written science fiction occurs in Robert Heinlein's *Stranger in a Strange Land* (1961). Valentine Smith, a human raised on Mars by Martians, returns to Earth, and very much like the mythical feral children emerging from the forest, brings with him the boon of his off-world innocence and wisdom with its power to transform Human society—which ultimately rejects his gift. In fact, Smith is a combination of Feral Child and, as a result of this innocence, another archetype, the Holy Fool. It isn't surprising that this character proved so popular with readers during the hippy years of the sixties and seventies when people were questioning the values of western civilization and advocating a return to simpler times.

Sometimes the "lost child" theme is disguised in a story, so that at first we may not see its connection with the trope. The distinguishing features to look for are, firstly, a child who is somehow "lost" to the society, who therefore possesses an innocence, a fresh way of seeing familiar things in that society, and second, a re-union or re-integration of some sort, which (usually) turns out to be unsuccessful. One such "disguised" story of a lost child occurs in Daniel Keyes' moving tale "Flowers for Algernon" (1959), later expanded into a novel of the same name). Charlie Gordon has not so much wandered away or been lost from his society as that he was never a fully functioning member of it from birth. Charlie, who is retarded, displays a sweet nature, lacking guile; mercilessly mocked by co-workers in the factory where he holds a menial job, he innocently joins in the laughter. "That made me laff," he writes in one of his *progris riports,* "Their really my friends and they like me" (p. 611). The subject of a questionable surgical experiment to raise his IQ, Charlie grows from retardation to genius. But in this state of advanced intelligence, he makes a profound discovery:

> The unforeseen development, which I have taken the liberty of calling the Algernon-Gordon Effect, is the logical extension of the entire intelligence speed-up. The hypothesis here proven may be described in the following terms: Artificially increased intelligence deteriorates at a rate of time directly proportional to the quantity of the increase. (p. 629)

As Charlie, the once "lost child" forecasts, the intelligence he has gained diminishes, and so does Charlie's potential value to his society; the experiment is unsuccessful.

The Russian team of brothers Boris and Arkady Strugatsky gave the feral child theme a science fictional setting in their novel *The Little One* (1971). Here, a young child, orphaned after his parents' spaceship crashes on an alien planet, is raised by aliens until the day a human expedition arrives and takes him back to Earth. Like many stories of feral children returning to civilization, this one portrays the attempt as unsuccessful.

Other times, lost child stories combine the dangers of the surrounding wild lands with folklore and fairy tales of the Old Folk, the faerie folk who abduct human children and raise them as their own, with thoroughly science fictional results. A notable example of such echoing of fairy tale themes occurs in Poul Anderson's story "The Queen of Air and Darkness" (1971), a tale of a colony planet where a human child is stolen from its mother by shadowy native inhabitants:

> Usually an outwayer family has given a tearful but undetailed account of their child who vanished and must have been stolen by the Old Folk.

> Sometimes, years later, they'd tell about glimpses
> of what they swore must have been the grown
> child, not really human any longer. (p. 698)

I remember in graduate seminars studying the difference between the European myth of the forest (we are surrounded by the menacing forces of nature and must endure) and the American myth of the frontier (we face the unknown and must advance), and how these referenced the historic situation that the cultures that gave rise to them were embedded in. The dark unknown of the universe lying outside our own well-lighted planet may have replaced the unknown terrors of the primeval forest just beyond the tiny village, but its message is essentially the same. In all that scary mystery there may be treasures of knowledge that we may, with good fortune, come to benefit from, but it isn't going to be easy. Nor may we always be able to recognize or nurture those returning travelers who seek to bring us the wisdom of their experiences.

The Fascination of Apocalypse

Recently, I had the opportunity to look over photos of the damage done by an earthquake that struck Long Beach in 1933. Toppled church spires, debris spilling over the roads, schools and businesses demolished, people sleeping in tents by the ruins. There's something compelling about other people's horrendous events, the greater the destruction the greater the fascination, just as long as we ourselves are safe. This has been the case at least since the unknown Israelite scribe set down the story of Noah's Ark that later became part of the Christian Old Testament, and we were hooked on tales of our—sometimes deserved—destruction as a race.

The Old Testament doesn't give the only account of an apocalyptic flood washing away humankind, nor does it give us the only survivor who goes on to repopulate the Earth. We find similar tales across the globe, from the Mesopotamian epic of Gilgamesh, through the Viking story of Ragnarök, to stories that appear in Hindu sacred texts. And the New Testament gives us the Book of Revelations with yet another depiction of Apocalypse. Myths from Greece and around the globe are not short of stories in which the gods capriciously, or as punishment for human hubris, blast whole societies back to their Stone Ages.

We humans seem to be morbidly fascinated with prophecies of our own destruction; our myths are full of them. This fascination probably stems from our knowledge of how close we always are to total annihilation in a frequently hostile natural world, something humankind has always understood. That we exist on the brink of the abyss is deeply engraved in our racial memory; catastrophe threatens around every bend in the road the tribe takes on its migration toward the future. We have always been at the mercy of floods, famines, droughts, tornadoes, earthquakes, and fierce predators. We sometimes overlook the fact that the great mythic Hero's Journey of Odysseus came at the close of the apocalyptic (at least to the Trojans) war between Greece and Troy. Homer's audiences must have been as captivated by that story of wrongdoing, revenge, and annihilation as they were by Odysseus's meanderings on the way home. The tribe's need to learn how to avoid destroying itself is primal; only after that is accomplished can its members settle down to the task of their own psychological growth.

To our ancestors, storytelling served two purposes, entertainment and education, both practical and religious. Flood myths are ubiquitous because floods themselves are, and so are myths of wrathful gods destroying tribes or whole nations. The causes and details may differ, but the underlying message is always the same: The tribe needs to *do something* to avoid a recurrence. The message doesn't have to be global apocalypse. *Puss-in-Boots,* a child's nursery tale, acclaims the perhaps legendary discovery that cats hunt rats, and rats carry the fleas that carry the plague virus. *Ergo*, the story tells us, against a backdrop of horse-drawn carts overflowing with dead victims on the streets of an increasingly deserted London, stop fearing cats as agents of the devil and put them to work hunting rats. The shiver and the message seem to compel readers in equal proportions.

Since Mary Shelley's *The Last Man* (1826), we've had some semblance of scientific underpinning to our dystopic visions. Sometimes the cause of our projected demise is that nightmare of the twentieth century, nuclear destruction. For instance, we can look at Nevil Shute's *On the Beach* (1957), where the last survivors contemplate their fate when the rest of the world has been annihilated, or David Brin's *The Postman* (1985), a tale of remnant populations trying to re-establish the trappings of civilization through the medium of a reluctant "postman" delivering mail in the system from before the holocaust. (An interesting story to complement Brin's tale of the postman is Connie Willis's "A Letter from the Clearys" (1982), where one such lost piece of mail finally finds its recipients after the apocalyptic event. They are none too pleased to be reminded of their previous, now lost forever, circumstances.) Leigh Brackett's *The Long Tomorrow* (1955) is another post-holocaust novel, where some struggle to reestablish civilization, and ironically, the technology that destroyed it. Sometimes it's a plague, natural or man-made, but preferably the latter for dramatic purposes, so the author can play on our sense of guilt. Consider Richard Matheson's *I Am Legend* (1964), Brian Aldiss's *Greybeard* (1964) where it's a plague of infertility that has doomed the human race, and also *Barefoot in the Head* (1969) where the plague has had a rather more malicious start. George R. Stewart's *Earth Abides* (1949) comes to mind for another example.

In *The Drowned World* (1962), J. G. Ballard gives us an echo of the flood myths in the melting of the polar caps as the cause of catastrophe, though this happens as the result of solar flares rather than as we might think today, global warming. Larry Niven and Jerry Pournelle use an asteroid strike as the cause of apocalypse in their collaboration *Lucifer's Hammer* (1977). A recent trilogy by Kim Stanley Robinson—*Forty Signs of Rain* (2004), *Fifty Degrees Below* (2005), and *Sixty Days and Counting* (2007)—realistically develops the disastrous results of human-influenced climate change. A similar fate for the world appears in Kate Wilhelm's *Juniper Time* (1979), where apocalypse comes through devastating drought. One of the most famous "end of humanity" tales, where the cause is alien in origin, is Arthur Clarke's *Childhood's End* (1953), the transcendent fate of the young is little consolation to those who are going to be left behind. Sometimes, the author chooses not to name the cause (although we can guess it is nuclear in origin) but to concentrate on the after-effects of destruction, for instance Cormac McCarthy's *The Road* (2006).

Occasionally, we find an apocalyptic novel putting the focus on what people will do in the face of impending doom, rather than on the nature of the catastrophe or the fate of the survivor's afterwards. Such a story is Ben Winters' *The Last Policeman* (2012), which is concerned more with a moral question than with the approach of the destructive asteroid. Indeed, how many of us would feel impelled to go about our regular duties—even if they benefit society—if we and society are headed for oblivion in the very near future?

These apocalyptic visions can act as deterrents—if we don't like the results of this thought experiment, we can choose to do something different. But some writers such as Roger Zelazny give us a more chilling scenario, one in which the choice may not be ours to make. In "The Game of Blood and Dust" (1975), we learn we are not the captains of our own fate, but rather the pawns of a couple of very powerful aliens whose godlike powers the Greeks would recognize very well:

They reentered the sequence…. Radio noises hummed about them. Satellites orbited the world. Highways webbed the continents…. Jets slid through the atmosphere…. Blood chuckled.

"You have to admit it was very close," said Dust. They regarded the world, its two and a half billions of people, their cities, their devices…

After a time, the inhabitant of the forward point spoke: "Best two out of three?"

"All right. I am Blood. I go first."

"And I am Dust. I follow you." (p. 444)

And—we may hope—tongue firmly in cheek, George Alec Effinger's story "All the Last Wars at Once" shows us the potential result of all our petty, dangerous squabbles. When people are allowed to go out and "get what [they] can for thirty days," thus allowing old divisions, resentments, and grudges to be settled by "bloody combat in the streets," eventually the only target left to destroy is themselves (p. 446).

So if descriptions of apocalypse are so numerous in the literature, how are we to make critical distinctions between them? Bigger weapons of mass destruction? Better methods of annihilating humanity? More gruesome descriptions of after-effects? All of those have had their day, and like all novel ideas, at first they are fresh and startling, then they become cliché, which is my basic complaint about Cormac McCarthy's excursion into genre writing, *The Road*, where the characters seem to react passively to their circumstances. For me, as for most science fiction readers, there has to be something more. It's a legitimate question to ask of an apocalyptic story: What did the survivors do? There have to be some survivors of this fictional apocalypse, or else there's no story, just a gruesome but essentially static picture. Readers want to see action on the part of those left behind—to co-opt a decidedly non-science fictional series of books that nevertheless do answer the question about what happened next. By contrast to McCarthy's road-trip novel, the recent *Soft Apocalypse* (2011) by Will McIntosh details what happens when society crumbles and resources we take for granted fail after the holocaust. McIntosh invites us along as a likable and believable group of ordinary folk try to survive in difficult circumstances; his characters may be as doomed in the long run as McCarthy's, but at least they are actively involved in seeking their own survival.

The extreme response to this question can be seen in Walter M. Miller's *A Canticle for Leibowitz,* which follows the survivors of nuclear catastrophe for centuries—all the way to the moment when humans seem on the verge of repeating the disaster. A high point of this novel is Miller's thesis that the Catholic church, guardian of knowledge through Europe's long centuries in the dark wasteland of Medieval superstition and ignorance, is the most likely organization to survive societal breakdown after a nuclear war, repeating its role as protector and promoter of the return to civilization. It also harbors the biggest threat of repeating the apocalyptic event.

Other novels examine the changes in society that evolve as a result of the disaster. Russell Hoban, in *Riddley Walker* (1980), explores—amongst other things—the extreme drift in language that might occur as a result of the disruption of communication. In a book where reading the text becomes an exercise in reader participation, much as it does in Anthony Burgess's *A Clockwork Orange* (1962), we encounter a well thought out description of linguistic change, both in structure and idiom. For example, where we today might say about a friend's attempt to send a message, "he phoned me"—or wrote or texted—Hoban's characters say "he pigeond me," a gem of an invention that tells so much more about the state of this civilization after the apocalypse than just the fact one character sent another a message.

Recently, I read one of the classics in this sub-genre that I had managed to miss, Pat Frank's *Alas, Babylon* (1959). Frank spends little time detailing the exact extent of the nuclear strikes around the globe that bring civilization to its knees. Instead, he's concerned with the reaction of one of the isolated, remnant populations in attempting to deal with the unthinkable. There's something reminiscent of the classic tv show "Father Knows Best" here, the characters being a trifle too resourceful at times, and too successful in restoring civility to a hard-scrabble life after the bomb:

> He must make a list of the things Helen and the children would need. He recalled that there was nothing stocked in the big kitchen downstairs, and little in the utility room except some steaks in the freezer and a few canned staples. My God, if there was going to be a war they'd need stocks of everything! (p. 19)

The tone here reflects the prevailing split of the fifties in America: fear of nuclear holocaust, and a strong belief that the family can conquer anything life throws at it. This philosophy may be a little hard to swallow for us in our jaded times, but as a story it satisfies because it shows the characters *doing* rather than simply *reacting*.

It's not just that science fiction readers tend to like robots and spaceships and aliens and terrible disasters— lots of mainstream-minded viewers also enjoy Hollywood's versions of these tropes. And I would certainly argue that it has little to do with appreciation of literary quality since some of the most popular tales are lacking in the department of sophisticated writing. The difference is that sf readers expect thought experiments; we want to take part in the story. We enjoy discussing the problems encountered by the characters as if they were real, and we like to debate the pros and cons of the solutions proposed. We approach such stories, especially apocalyptic or dystopic ones, as more than just a way to pass a few hours of idle time, or as a means to give us vicarious chills that we can immediately forget as we go about our safe and rather mundane lives. We want to learn from the possible futures we're introduced to, not just be appalled or terrorized. Will unchecked population expansion lead to the overcrowding of John Brunner's *Stand on Zanzibar* (1968) or the thinly-disguised cannibalism of Harry Harrison's *Make Room! Make Room!* (1966) or Margaret Atwood's eerily prophetic tale of the demise of women's rights in *The Handmaid's Tale* (1985) or J. G. Ballard's story of overcrowding, "Billenium" (1961), which is all the more chilling because humans seem to be adapting to it? Science fiction stories often yield up their profoundest riches when we approach them by contemplating, *If this goes on.* And then we ask, *Do we really want that?* I find that a deeply mythic response.

So what purpose does an exhibition of decades-old earthquake photos serve for the viewers? I'll answer that right after I check my earthquake supplies.

The Persistence
of the Numinous

On the bluff in Long Beach, facing the Pacific across busy Ocean Boulevard, there's a well-kept shrine to the Virgin Mary. A rainbow of flowers blooms at her feet, replenished every day by admirers. Next to the shrine there's a red-tiled monastery, but it's Buddhist now, not Roman Catholic. For forty years, a group of Carmelite nuns made their home here, devoted to a life of solitude and contemplation, but eventually the boulevard became too busy and too noisy for them to continue. So they sold their convent to the Sagely order of Buddhist monks and retreated to a quieter place. Only one requirement was asked of the monks, that they not remove the shrine of the Virgin Mary. "We are delighted to keep her," said the monks when the City of Ten Thousand Buddhas bought the convent. "After all, we know Mary as Guanji Bodhisattva." The name is perhaps more familiar to us as Kwan Yin, goddess of mercy and compassion.

The story doesn't stop there. This particular image of Mary is *Maria Stella Maris*, or Mary Star of the Sea, patron of all who venture upon the wide waters. The symbol that marks her in this aspect is a shell; thus the statue is backed by a large, open clam shell. But wait a minute, wasn't there a myth of a Greek goddess who rose from the sea on a shell? Indeed: Aphrodite, goddess of love. So our shrine seems to recognize three sacred females, not one: Aphrodite, Kwan Yin, and Mary. The plethora of identities for the shrine doesn't seem to bother the faithful who stop by. And even non-religious passers-by often express their fondness for the site, although they might have trouble explaining why.

I have a feeling Jung would've understood. The Swiss psychologist might have commented that worship of the Great Mother—whose daughter was Aphrodite—appears to be alive and well in Long Beach today. At any rate, the shrine seems to be a good example of the persistence of the numinous in our secular society. The hallmark of numinosity, as Jung explained it, is that its effect can't be completely understood by intellect alone; it's that wholly other moment when we experience something we can't quite put into words. We end up using terms like "transcendent" or "holy," though the effect is not limited to the religious experience; even the agnostic Carl Sagan tried to capture the effects of the numinous in the universe. At its most intense, numinous experience seems to induce the perception of an archetype from the collective unconscious: in the case of our shrine, the female form of the deity. Such archetypes inspire a kind of mystical awe, even though as rational twenty-first-century citizens of the world we may not acknowledge the experience.

Could a similar response, perhaps as old as humanity, be happening in books and movies whose appeal seems out of proportion to the brilliance or originality of the plot or the beauty of the writing? Is it possible that in the modern world we still need this experience and will take it wherever we find it? In *The Writer's Journey* (1985), Christopher Vogler explains that the success of movies as varied as *High Noon* (1952), *The Wizard of Oz* (1939), and *Star Wars* depends on their utilization of one particular archetype, the Hero who sets out on a perilous journey. In other words, we side with Luke Skywalker because we identify unconsciously with the archetype he portrays: the stranger, the outsider, called from obscurity to oust the bad guys and right society's wrongs and then walk away from the triumph. The mythic Hero often pays a terrible price at the end—Orpheus was torn to pieces by his ecstatic followers; the obscure carpenter from Nazareth was crucified. Even in the frenetic twenty-first century, something deep in us responds to this ancient pattern when we encounter it.

Perhaps this might explain the success of books like Orson Scott Card's *Ender's Game* (1985), which can be criticized for its scientific illogic or its amoral philosophy, but still has the haunting power to grab readers. Ender Wiggins is certainly an innocent outsider called on to save his society. Likewise, in J. K. Rowling's Harry Potter series, dismissed by some as derivative, we find a version of the same myth of the unlikely person called to right a wrong. On some level we obviously aren't reading for logic or originality; our response is to something much more ancient. For the sake of the hard-to-explain but powerful emotional experience we receive from stories such as these, we're more than willing to suspend our disbelief.

Shakespeare understood this. That's why it's not important that his plots and characters were recognizably borrowed from other sources. His genius was to endow them with a touch of the numinous. Try putting the plot of any of his plays into a paragraph or two and you'll find the difference between the story and the effect the play has on the audience. Maybe this explains why Prospero's speech in Act Four of *The Tempest* (perhaps his most deeply numinous play), evokes the non-rational sadness of being banished from fairyland, a paradise lost, a country of myth that lies just over the hill in our collective unconscious:

> Our revels now are ended. These our actors,
> As I foretold you, were all spirits, and
> Are melted into air, into thin air,
> And like the baseless fabric of this vision,
> The cloud-capped towers, the gorgeous palaces,
> The solemn temples, the great globe itself,
> Yea, all which it inherit, shall dissolve;
> And like this insubstantial pageant faded,
> Leave not a rack behind.

So we stand on the bluffs before this shrine of Mary, Kwan Yin, or Aphrodite, and experience the tingle of the ineffable. The symbol inspires the intense feeling that we know something that our rational brains insist we don't know and maybe doesn't even exist outside of our dreams, and we sense that we would be poorer without it. Is it any surprise that a literature about the future should make use of such a powerful tool?

On the subject of science fiction's mythological roots, James Blish once declared that myth is static, unlike science fiction, which, he said, assumes continuous change. It seems to me that Blish is confusing the *medium* of myth with the *message*. The power of the archetypal myth of Icarus is not that it's a story about a young man who one day flew too close to the sun on waxen wings, but lies instead in its message about the eternal danger of being so full of ourselves and our own abilities that we ignore advice and fatally overlook our limitations. It would be hard to find a more relevant myth for our spacefaring age!

If the purpose of myth is to convey the eternal truths of the human embedded in the world, science fiction is frequently equally didactic. The starting point of science fiction, "If this goes on…" carries an unstated corollary: If you don't like the look of the future world, do something to avoid it now.

Works Cited

Aldiss, Brian. "Barefoot in the Head," *New Worlds*. 1969.

———. *Greybeard*. London: Faber and Faber, 1964.

Anderson, Poul. "Goat Song," *Science Fiction: Contemporary Mythology*. New York: Harper and Row, 1960.

———. "The Queen of Air and Darkness," *Great Science Fiction of the 20th Century*. New York: Avenel Books, 1971.

———. *Tau Zero*. New York: Doubleday, 1970.

Asimov, Isaac. "The Bicentennial Man," *Stellar-2*. New York: Ballantine, 1976.

———. *I, Robot*. New York: Gnome Press, 1950.

Atwood, Margaret. *The Handmaid's Tale*. Toronto: McClelland and Stewart, 1985.

Bacigalupi, Paolo. *The Windup Girl*. San Francisco: Nightshade Books, 2009.

Ballard, J. G. "Billenium," *Science Fiction: Contemporary Mythology*. New York: Harper and Row, 1961.

———. *The Drowned World*. New York: Ballantine, 1962.

Baum, Frank L. *The Wonderful Wizard of Oz*, Chicago: George M. Hill Company, 1900.

Beagle, Peter. *Tamsin*. New York: Roc, 1999.

Benford, Gregory. *Across The Sea of Suns*. New York: Simon and Schuster, 1984.

——. *Against Infinity.* New York: Harper Voyager, 1983.

——. *Great Sky River.* New York: Bantam, 1987.

——. *Tides of Light. New York: Bantam,* 1989.

—— and Gordon Ecklund. *If the Stars Are Gods.* New York: Berkeley, 1977.

Bettelheim, Bruno. *The Uses of Enchantment.* New York: Random House, 1975.

Brackett, Leigh. *The Long Tomorrow.* New York: Doubleday, 1955.

Bradbury, Ray, *Dandelion Wine.* New York: Bantam, 1959.

——. *The Illustrated Man.* New York: Doubleday, 1951.

Brin, David. *Earth.* New York: Bantam Books, 1990.

——. *The Postman.* New York: Bantam Books, 1985.

Brunner, John. *Stand on Zanzibar.* London: Doubleday, 1968.

Burgess, Anthony. *A Clockwork Orange.* London: Heinemann, 1962.

Butler, Octavia. "Bloodchild," *Science Fiction: The SFRA Anthology.* New York: Harper and Row, 1984.

Campbell, Joseph. *The Hero with a Thousand Faces.* New Jersey, Princeton University Press, 1949.

Card, Orson Scott. *Ender's Game.* New York: Tor Books, 1985.

Carr, Terry. "The Dance of the Changer and the Three." *Science Fiction: Contemporary   Mythology.* New York: Harper and Row, 1968.

Clarke, Arthur C. *2001: A Space Odyssey* (expanded from "The Sentinel, " 1948). London: Hutchinson; New York: New American Library, 1968.

——. *Childhood's End.* London: Ballantine, 1953.

——. *The Fountains Of Paradise.* London: Gollancz, 1979.

———. "The Star," *Infinity Science Fiction Magazine.* 1955.

Clement, Hal. *Mission of Gravity.* New York: Doubleday, 1954.

Conrad, Joseph. "Heart of Darkness," *Blackwoods Magazine.* 1899.

Crichton, Michael. *Jurassic Park.* London: Knopf, 1990.

Crowley, John. *Aegypt.* New York: Bantam, 1987.

De Camp, L. Sprague. "Judgment Day," *Astounding Science Fiction Magazine.* 1955.

Delany, Samuel. *Nova.* New York: Doubleday, 1968.

De Lint, Charles. *Jack the Giant-Killer.* New York: Ace, 1987.

Del Rey, Lester. "Helen O'Loy," *Astounding Science Fiction Magazine.* 1938.

Dick, Phillip K. *The Three Stigmata of Palmer Erdritch.* New York: Doubleday, 1965.

Dowling, Terry. *Blue Tyson.* North Adelaide, South Australia: Aphelion Publications, 1992.

Effinger, George Alec. "All the Last Wars at Once," *Science Fiction: Contemporary Mythology.* New York: Harper and Row, 1978.

Eliade, Mircea. *Myth and Reality.* New York: Harper and Row, 1963.

Eliot, T. S. "Hamlet and His Problems," *The Sacred Wood.* New York: Knopf, 1921.

Erdrich, Louise. *The Antelope Wife.* New York: Harper Collins, 1998.

Estés, Clarissa Pinkola. *Women Who Run With the Wolves.* New York: Ballantine Books, 1992.

Farmer, Philip Jose. *Riverworld* (series). New York: Putnam, 1971-1983.

Finch, Sheila. "Stranger Than Imagination Can," *The Guild of Xenolinguists*. Urbana: Golden Gryphon Press, 2007.

———. "No Brighter Glory," *Fantasy and Science Fiction*. April 1999.

Fowles, John. *The Magus*. London: Little, Brown and Company, 1966.

Frank, Pat. *Alas, Babylon*. New York: Bantam Books, 1959.

Gernsback, Hugo. "Ralph 24C1 4c1+," *Modern Electronics*. 1911.

Gilbert, Sandra M. "Rider Haggard's Heart of Darkness," *Coordinates: Placing Science Fiction and Fantasy*. Carbondale: Southern Illinois University Press, 1983.

Golding, William. *Lord of the Flies*. London: Faber and Faber, 1954.

Grahame, Kenneth, *The Wind in the Willows*. London: Methuen, 1908.

Griffith, Nicola. *Slow River*. New York: Ballantine, 1995.

Harrison, Harry. *Make Room! Make Room!* New York: Doubleday, 1966.

Heinlein, Robert, *Stranger in a Strange Land*. New York: Putnam, 1961.

Herbert, Frank. *Whipping Star*. New York: Putnam, 1970.

———. *Dune*. New York: Chilton Books, 1965.

Hoban, Russell. *Riddley Walker*. New York: Summit Books, 1980.

Hoyle, Fred, *The Black Cloud*. London: Heinemann, 1957.

Huxley, Aldous. *Brave New World*. London: Chatto and Windus, 1932.

Johnson, Kij. *The Fox Woman*. New York: Tor Books, 2000.

Jung, Carl Gustav. *Psychology and Religion*. New Haven: Yale University Press, 1953.

Keyes, Daniel. "Flowers for Algernon," *The Science Fiction Hall of Fame*. New York: Avon Books, 1970.

Lee, Tanith. *The Silver Metal Lover*. New York: DAW, 1981.

Le Guin, Ursula. *The Left Hand of Darkness*. New York: Ace, 1969.

———. *The Word For World Is Forest*. New York: Putnam, 1976.

———. "Winter's King," *Great Science Fiction of the 20ᵗʰ Century*. New York: Avenel Books, 1969.

———. "Vaster Than Empires and More Slow," *Science Fiction: A Historical Anthology*. Oxford: Oxford University Press, 1983.

———. *A Wizard of Earthsea*. New York: Bantam, 1968.

Leinster, Murray. "The Lonely Planet," *Thrilling Wonder Stories*. 1949.

Lem, Stanislaw. *Solaris*. New York: Walker, 1970.

Lewis, C. S. *Perelandra*. London: Bodley Head, 1943.

———. *The Lion, The Witch and The Wardrobe*. London: Geoffrey Bles, 1950.

Lovelock, James and Lynn Margulis. *The First Gaia Conference*. San Diego, CA, 1988.

Marlowe, Christopher. *Doctor Faustus,* 1588.

Martin, George R. R. "The Sand Kings," *Omni*. 1979.

Matheson, Richard. *I Am Legend*. Robbinsdale MN: Gold Medal, 1954.

MacLeish, Archibald, "Ars Poetica," *Poetry Magazine*. June 1926.

McCarthy, Cormac. *The Road*. New York: Knopf, 2006.

McDonald, Ian. "The Djinn's Wife," *Cyberabad Days*. Amhurst: Prometheus Books, 2009.

———. *River of Gods.* Amhurst: Prometheus Books, 2007.

McIntosh, Will. *Soft Apocalypse.* San Francisco: Nightshade, 2011.

McGilchrist, Iain, *The Master and His Emissary.* New Haven, CT: Yale University Press, 2009.

Menzies, Gavin. *1421: The Year China Discovered America.* New York: William Morrow, 2004.

Miéville, China. *The Scar.* London: Macmillan, 2002.

Miller, Walter. *A Canticle for Leibowitz,* Philadelphia: J.B. Lippincott, 1960.

More, Sir Thomas. *Utopia,* 1516.

Moore, C. L. "No Woman Born," *Science Fiction: The SFRA Anthology.* New York: Harper and Row, 1944.

Mosquito Coast, The. Directed by Peter Weir. (Based on the book by Paul Theroux). Burbank, CA: Warner Brothers, 1986.

Niven, Larry, and Jerry Pournelle. *Lucifer's Hammer.* Los Angeles: Playboy Press, 1977.

Nourse, Alan E. "Brightside Crossing," *Science Fiction: Contemporary Mythology.* New York: Harper and Row, 1978.

O'Brien, Tim. *The Things They Carried.* Boston: Houghton Mifflin Harcourt, 1986.

Orwell, George. *1984.* London: Secker and Warburg, 1949.

Pangborn, Edgar. *Davy.* New York: St. Martin's Press, 1964.

Piercy, Marge. *Woman on the Edge of Time.* New York: Knopf, 1976.

Priest, Christopher. *The Islanders.* London: Gollancz, 2011.

Pullman, Phillip. *Count Karlstein*. London: Chatto and Windus, 1982.

Roberts, Adam. *Jack Glass*. London: Gollancz, 2012.

Robinson, Kim Stanley. *Forty Signs of Rain*. New York: Bantam Spectra, 2004.

——. *Fifty Degrees Below*. New York: Bantam Spectra, 2005.

——. *Sixty Days and Counting*. New York: Bantam Spectra, 2007.

Roshwald, Mordecai. *Dreams and Nightmares: Science and Technology in Myth and Fiction*. Jefferson, NC: McFarland and Company, 2008.

Rowling, J.K. *Harry Potter*. London: Bloomsbury Publishing, 1997.

Russ, Joanna. *The Female Man*. New York: Bantam, 1975.

Russell, Mary Doria. *The Sparrow*. New York, Ballantine Books, 1996.

Shakespeare, William. *The Tempest,* 1611.

Shelley, Mary. *Frankenstein*. Boston: St. Martin's Press, 1992.

Schenck, Hilbert. *A Rose for Armageddon*. New York; Bantam, 1982.

Shute, Neville. *On the Beach*. London: Heinemann, 1957.

Silverberg, Robert. *Downward to the Earth*. New York: Doubleday, 1970.

Spinrad, Norman. *The Void Captain's Tale*. New York: Simon and Schuster, 1983.

Stewart, George. *Earth Abides*. New York: Random House, 1949.

Stevenson, Robert Louis. *The Strange Case of Dr Jekyll and Mr Hyde*. London: Longmans Green and Co. 1886.

Straley, John. *The Woman Who Married a Bear.* New York: Soho Press, 1992.

Straub, Peter. *Shadowland.* New York: Coward McCann, 1980.

Strugatsky, Boris and Arkady. *The Little One.* London: Macmillan, 1971.

Sturgeon, Theodore. "Affair with a Green Monkey," *Venture Science Fiction Magazine,* 1953.

———. "Memorial," *Science Fiction: Modern Mythology.* New York: Harper and Row, 1946.

———. "Microcosmic God," *The Science Fiction Hall of Fame.* New York: Avon, 1971.

Sugden, John. *Sir Francis Drake.* New York: Henry Holt, 1990.

Tepper, Sheri, *Grass.* London: Gollancz, 1989.

Thomas, Dylan. *Under Milk Wood.* London: J.M. Dent, 1954.

Tiptree, James, Jr. "The Women Men Don't See," *Great Science Fiction of the 20th Century.* New York: Avenel, 1973.

Tolkien, J. R. R. *Lord of the Rings.* London: Allen and Unwin, 1954.

Van Vogt, A. E. *The Voyage of the Space Beagle.* New York: Simon and Schuster, 1950.

Verne, Jules. *Twenty Thousand Leagues Under the Sea.* Paris: Hetzel, 1870.

Vinge, Joan. *The Snow Queen.* New York: Warner Books, 1980.

Vogler, Christopher. *The Writer's Journey.* Los Angeles: Michael Wiese Production, 1985.

Vonnegut, Kurt. *Cat's Cradle.* New York: Holt Rinehart and Winston, 1963.

Watson, Ian. *The Gardens of Delight.* London: Gollancz, 1980.

Weinbaum, Stanley. *A Martian Odyssey, and Other Science Fiction Tales*. New York: Hyperion. 1934.

Wells, H. G. *The Island of Doctor Moreau,* in *Making Humans*. Boston: Houghton Mifflin Company, 2003.

———. *The War of the Worlds*. London: Heinemann, 1898.

Wilhelm, Kate. *Juniper Time*. New York: Harper and Row, 1979.

Willis, Connie. "A Letter From the Clearys," *Asimov's Science Fiction Magazine,* 1982.

Winters, Ben. The Last Policeman. Philadelphia: Quirk Books, 2012.

Wilson, G. Willow. Alif the Unseen. New York: Grove Press, 2012.

Zelazny, Roger. "The Game of Blood and Dust," Science Fiction: Modern Mythology. New York: Harper and Row, 1975.

———. "A Rose for Ecclesiastes," *Science Fiction: The SFRA Anthology*. New York: Harper and Row, 1963.

———. *Lord of Light*. New York: Doubleday, 1967.

Zoline, Pamela. "The Heat Death of the Universe," *New Worlds Magazine*, 1967.

Author Biography

Sheila Finch was born and raised in London, UK. Her undergraduate career started at Bishop Otter College, an Anglican women's college in Sussex that has now morphed into the co-ed University of Chichester. Upon graduation, she taught for one year in a primary school in London's docklands, a slum in those days, but now home to multimillionaires with yachts. After marriage to an American, she lived in Indiana for five years, doing graduate work in Medieval Literature and Linguistics at Indiana University. Moving to San Luis Obispo in the sixties, she found life on the West Coast to her liking. She taught creative writing and the literature of science fiction at El Camino College for thirty years. She's retired now and lives in Long Beach with two cats. She has three daughters, eight grandchildren, and one great-grandchild.

Sheila is the author of eight science fiction novels; the first published, *Infinity's Web*, won the Compton Crook Award, and a Young Adult novel, *Tiger in the Sky*, earned the San Diego Book Award. Numerous short stories have appeared in *Fantasy & Science Fiction, Amazing, Asimov's, Fantasy Book*, and many anthologies. A collection of the "lingster" stories about the young men and women trained as translators and interpreters to aliens appeared as *The Guild of Xenolinguists*; one of them, "Reading The Bones," won a Nebula. She has also published non-fiction about writing and science fiction.

Her musings can be found on Facebook and LiveJournal, and her website is at: www.sff.net/people/sheila-finch/.